Driving Digital Transformation in Developing Nations

Nagy K. Hanna

Driving Digital Transformation in Developing Nations

Case Studies

palgrave
macmillan

Nagy K. Hanna
Bethesda, MD, USA

ISBN 978-3-031-54572-6 ISBN 978-3-031-54573-3 (eBook)
https://doi.org/10.1007/978-3-031-54573-3

This Palgrave Macmillan imprint is published by the registered company Springer Nature Switzerland AG
The registered company address is: Gewerbestrasse 11, 6330 Cham, Switzerland

Paper in this product is recyclable.

Foreword

"Digitalise or die" should be the twenty-first-century motto of public and private sector organizations around the world. In the last decade, digital technologies have become pervasive, resulting in greater speed, efficiency, productivity, customer interaction, and transparency, while creating new opportunities. Organizations that have not adopted digital technologies or have been slow in doing so are losing the race to those who have embraced them.

While digital transformation is a matter of survival in the business world, at the country level, it is of great importance to national governments and a powerful tool for better governance. Digital technology transforms citizen services while access to government information (guaranteed, in some cases, by law) makes for better transparency and accountability, adding a key component to democratic governance. Artificial intelligence is increasingly used in social services such as health care, in the prediction of disease spread, in weather forecasts, cyber fraud detection, and so on.

Many new services have been enabled by digital technologies. India, a developing country that has leveraged digital technologies as a development tool, has implemented many effective applications. For example, Aadhaar, a biometrics identity app, has provided digital identity to 99% of India's adult population. The Universal Payments Interface connects multiple accounts into a single mobile app, similarly, doctors anywhere can access health records (granted patient permission), conduct teleconsultations, and receive payment.

At the same time, the rapid expansion of the telecommunication network for mobile telephony, combined with business model innovation to drive down voice and data rates, has led to a mobile revolution with over 1.1 billion wireless connections. A government initiative to ensure bank accounts for all has resulted in 460 million new accounts enabling direct transfer of funds (scholarships, pensions, subsidies, loans) to the beneficiary's bank account, ensuring transparency and minimizing corruption.

India has also created a Public Digital Infrastructure—a number of open-source platforms for application development.

These kinds of applications enable transparent and efficient government while easing the life of citizens. Importantly, the appropriate use of digital technology can help bridge the divides between the rich and the poor; the illiterate/semi-literate and the educated; urban and rural; big buyers and small producers; bureaucrats and citizens. By empowering those at the bottom, it can help eliminate poverty and create new opportunities.

Digital technologies also enable a mutually reinforcing cycle between new application development and the growth of a national software or electronics manufacturing industry—thus accelerating economic development. India, for example, has developed a business model which enabled it to create a global outsourcing-offshoring market. It had the advantages of a large talent base, low costs, explicit policies to nurture a digital transformation ecosystem, close collaboration between industry and government (thanks to NASSCOM), business leaders with a vision, and a supportive political and administrative leadership. Regulation was "light touch." As a result, India now has a USD 200 billion IT software and services industry, which provides direct employment to over 4 million people.

An important contributor to the growth of this industry was a 1990 World Bank study as part of a USD 250 million project to assist India in the development of electronics manufacturing, engineering education, research, and training. A million dollars was allocated to support the creation of a national strategy for the software services industry. It is amazing how this study catalyzed the first steps in building a vision and a road map for the growth of India's successful software and services industry. The key driver of this effort from the World Bank was Nagy

Hanna. The initial target then was to go from USD 50 million to a billion in 5 years. In a few years, this industry will hit the USD 300 billion mark!

Digital technologies not only offer immense opportunities, but also pose substantial risks. An issue of growing concern is cybercrime, both domestic and trans-national. While national laws seek to handle the former, the latter lacks clear international law. Such crime has progressed from affecting individuals to organizations, to countries. Also, there is growing unease with the power that tech giants have as a result of new technologies like AI, which enable the use of data to predict and influence behavior. In all the excitement about digital technology, it is important to minimize these dangers.

Countries see digital transformation as the way forward. For many developing countries it is an opportunity to overcome slow development and make a quantum leap. Hanna's case studies of India and Sri Lanka offer glimpses of how digital technologies can transform entire countries. His unique first-hand experiences demonstrate a holistic understanding of the complexities involved and shed light on the inner workings of the digital transformation ecosystem.

Understanding the drivers, opportunities, and challenges of the digital era is key to success in digital transformation. While the context and technologies keep changing, there is much to be learned from experience. It is always an invaluable guide. Hanna's experience provides exceptional insights. His work over the last five decades has increasingly focused on the digital space and his rich personal recollections of working in different countries are full of rare perspectives across cultures and governments. As one reads through the book—part autobiographical memoir, part professional journey, and part a deep analytical look at how multilateral agencies approach ICT-driven development, one understands Hanna's personal commitment to poverty alleviation. His empathy with his clients makes for exceptional focus, often spurring conflict with the "pragmatists" at the Bank. Like all pioneers, he was probably ahead of the times.

For a vast number of countries, donor assistance often shapes—and even dictates—projects. For policymakers in these countries, Hanna's insights into the inner workings of major donor agencies will be invaluable. He also proposes ways to accelerate digital learning and innovation within and among aid agencies to harness the digital revolution for development.

As digital technology sweeps the world, how organizations and countries adapt to technological change and how quickly they benefit from it becomes key to their competitiveness, and more broadly—to successful development, poverty elimination, and the achievement of SDG goals. Hanna's book is a useful guide for all those involved and interested in these tasks.

Gurgaon, India

Kiran Karnik
Author, and Former President,
NASSCOM

Acknowledgements

I am indebted to Anil Srivastava for inspiring me to write this memoir. Also thanks to Kiran Karnik for writing the preface.

I am grateful to Asya Rudkovskaya for her role as lead editor and thoughtful commentator.

My advocacy meeting with Kristalina Georgieva, then the CEO of the World Bank, was brief but influenced her decision to elevate the digital development function at the World Bank. Thanks to Jim Wolfensohn, then Bank President, Mohamed Muhsin, then CIO, and Praful Patel, then regional VP, who gave me the opportunity to collaborate with Sri Lankan policy makers on a pioneering digital transformation project.

I am grateful to Shinji Asanuma, Robert Picciotto, and Paul Isenman, as they generously shared their insights. Thanks to colleagues who influenced my thinking and commented on my drafts: Luci Abrahams, Klaus Tilmes, Tim Kelly, Peter Knight, Carlo Rossotto, Samia Melhem, Eduardo Talero, and Nigel Cameron. Also grateful to all who gave me their endorsements.

My learning journey through economic development in general and digital development assistance in particular has been shaped by many colleagues at the World Bank, policy makers in developing countries, and academics at universities and thinktanks.

Among World Bank leaders and colleagues who influenced my journey, I wish to mention: Mahmoud Mohieldin, Sanjay Pradhan, Peter Harrold, Deepak Mishra, Boutheina Guermazi, Christine Qiang, Philippe Dongier,

Shashank Ojha, Nimrod Raphaeli, Mahfouz Tadros, Ram Agarwala, Khalid Siraj, Dan Ritchie, H. Kohli, Mark Baird, Randeep Sudan, Shaku Gunaratne, Ian Scott, Chuck Zeigler, Helen Vazquez, Peter Scherer, Robert Schware, Carl Dahlman, Oleg Petrov, Carlos Braga, Sandra Sargent, Soniya Carvalho, and Miguel Schloss.

I owe debt to many senior policy makers and development practitioners in developing countries so I only mention those from India and Sri Lanka, the two country case studies: Milinda Moragoda, Eran Wickramaratne, Sam Pitroda, R. Chandrasekhar, Satya Narayanan, F.C.Kohli, K. Roy Paul, Saurabh Srivastava, N. Seshagiri, N. Vittal, Dewang Mehta, Harish Mehta, Lalit Weeratunga, Manju Haththotuwa, Reshan Dewapura, Jayantha Fernando, Wasantha Deshapriya, and Rohan Samarajiva.

Among thought leaders and academics who influenced my thinking I wish to mention: Vint Cerf, Richard Heeks, Robert Wade, Sandor Boyson, Elias Carayannis, Carlota Perez, Ernest Wilson, Dani Rodrik, Albert Hirschman, David Ellerman, Devish Kapur, Mike Porter, and Gunnar Myrdal.

Special thanks to Palgrave's editorial and Springer's production teams for quality work.

Not all of the above agree with my conclusions. I thank them all, without implicating them.

Last but not least, I am indebted to my wife Linda, and son James for bearing my absences while I spent disproportionate time at work and away from home on field missions.

Introduction

The digital revolution is creating unprecedented opportunities and challenges for economic development. Developing countries and aid agencies must embrace digital technologies and reinvent public policies and strategies for digital transformation to tackle interrelated grand development challenges: growing poverty and inequality, hunger and food insecurity, jobs and unemployment, health and pandemics, access to education, governance and corruption, conflicts and security, and water scarcity and climate change. Digital technology, or what has been traditionally called, information and communication technology (ICT) is a general-purpose technology that can be harnessed to provide innovative, powerful, and smart solutions across all sectoral and cross-sectoral challenges.

I take a holistic view of digital transformation. I propose an integrated framework that conceives digital transformation as both an *ecosystem* and a *process*. Digital transformation is about using digital technologies to initiate and support deep and sustainable change in structures and processes, modes of production and consumption, value creation from available resources, and/or substantial increases in access to and use of data and knowledge. It is carried out at many levels, including organizations, economic sectors, government functions, cities, and communities. It is also about the restructuring or transforming of whole economies.

Digital transformation is not just about access to digital technology by individual users. It is about learning to drive digital transformation by the whole society, especially if its full benefits were to be reaped. That means building and orchestrating collateral cultural, sociopolitical, institutional, and organizational changes. It is about building and transforming sociotechnical systems at scale.

A digital transformation ecosystem would include enabling policies and regulations, national information and communication infrastructures, data assets and infrastructure, digital competencies, public digital platforms, digital identification infrastructure, digital innovation and entrepreneurship ecosystems, and the interactions and partnerships among these foundations. These ecosystem foundations are shared among digital technologies, including the recent wave of AI-induced transformations. They are crosscutting enablers and building blocks for digital transformation and services at economy-wide or societal scale (World Bank, 2016, 2024; Hanna, 2016).

This book focuses on frameworks, tools, and examples of digital transformation at the country, government, city, regional, and economic sector levels. It draws lessons for country policymakers and local stakeholders to guide further digital transformation at all these levels.

The book draws on my personal experience in working with many client countries. It also corroborates and draws on relatively recent economic growth research that has given due attention to governance, institutions, and leadership (Growth Commission on Growth and Development, 2008; Acemoğlu and Robinson, 2012).

Country lessons of experience and growing political economy research show the critical roles that good governance, leadership, and institutions play in securing sustainable and inclusive development. As a new and cross-cutting process, digital transformation calls for transformative leadership, reformed institutions, good governance, public-private partnerships, and new cross-sectoral competencies. The economic return from investment in digital infrastructure depends on these sociopolitical factors, perhaps much more than investments in traditional infrastructures.

This book, on "Driving digital transformation for developing nations: case studies" and its companion book on "Economic development in the digital age" are about harnessing the digital revolution by countries, aid agencies, and development practitioners. In the companion book, I share my long struggles for reforming and innovating development practice—primarily concerning the challenges and opportunities arising from the recent digital revolution—in the pursuit of the mission of eliminating global poverty and securing inclusive and sustainable prosperity in a livable environment.

Book Organization

My work in the nascent field of digital transformation has taken me through periods of exploration, learning, fulfillment, and growth, but also fear and frustration, bordering on cynicism. It was often difficult to stay focused on addressing urgent client needs in line with my ideals and values while working with weak and often corrupt governments and dealing with the limitations of global aid agencies.

I reflect upon what motivated me to write this book in light of the many challenges facing humanity today: from climate change to growing inequality. I share my early fascination with economic planning models and their application in technical assistance to the Sudan. I then share my experiences as I served in various roles and contexts at the Bank and grew my understanding of the actual and potential roles of digital technologies in development. I recall my work in Indonesia and Palestine-Israel that helped me appreciate the demand side of information technologies and drove me to focus on improving the Bank's practice in technical assistance, institutional development, technology, and knowledge transfer.

In this book, I synthesize my experience in assisting countries, cities, and regions to digitally transform. I focus on two in-depth case studies where Bank assistance was influential. In India, back in 1990, the Bank financed a study of its software export strategy when the industry was still in its infancy. The demonstrated impact of this technical assistance suggests lessons for collaborative and catalytic roles for aid agencies. Building on this momentum, I worked with local stakeholders on a proposal for the Bank to finance a comprehensive strategy and investment program for integrating digital technology into India's development strategy (Hanna, 1994).

In a follow-up chapter, I describe my team's efforts to get the Executive Board of the Bank to approve financial and technical assistance to a new e-Sri Lanka program, the Bank's first holistic digital transformation investment. It was a pioneering program that was met by many institutional hurdles. It started under very difficult conditions, with no digital leadership, stable governance, or Bank readiness. Despite demonstrated achievements, Bank rigidities have since slowed the mainstreaming of holistic digital development assistance.

Two follow-up chapters explore two broad themes: *transforming government* (demand for good government, DFGG) and *smart cities*. In an era of growing political and economic polarization, can the DFGG movement strengthen the demand for transparent, responsive, and effective government? In view of growing urbanization and concerns about climate change, can smart city applications help city leaders and stakeholders manage these challenges in spite of turf rivalries? I explore how digital technologies can help develop responsive government and sustainable cities.

A follow-up chapter focuses on digital transformation at the sector level, selecting the health sector, its challenges and opportunities. It shares lessons of experience on how to harness digital technology to create a health learning system.

Next chapter compares the ways countries adopt national digital transformation strategies to advance economic development goals. Much can be learned from diverse country experiences. While national ambitions and goals for pursuing digital transformation may vary, key foundations and dynamics are shared. They present a rich learning agenda for practitioners. I draw lessons of experience from pioneering countries for policymakers and business leaders, and for educators and researchers to develop diagnostic tools and conceptual frameworks to advance the nascent discipline of digital transformation.

The book concludes with a synthesis of my experience in economy-wide digital transformation. How can policymakers and development practitioners harness the digital revolution to deliver significant and equitable benefits to developing countries? How should digital development strategies be pursued at the economy, government, and city levels?

Lessons of experience are organized into five fundamental challenges: enabling holistic and sustained transformational change; empowerment and ownership; leadership, institutions, and human resources; experimenting, learning, and evaluating; and inclusion and diffusion. They apply equally to practitioners like myself, and to countries and aid agencies. The book suggests how these challenges should be addressed by policymakers of developing countries and their counterparts in aid agencies.

Praise for *Driving Digital Transformation in Developing Nations*

"This book, written by prolific author and development intellectual, had my attention from the first page to the last. He has the uncanny ability to see into institutions deeply and to observe digital transformation processes intensely, and to express these insights in ways that enable the reader to see almost as deeply. In this book, Nagy Hanna looks into his own institution, the World Bank and offers analysis of its digital transformation journey, side by side with his own personal journey. He introduces us to brief country narratives from the digital transformation journeys of India, Sri Lanka and Kenya, and a few of the emerging smart city stories: Rio, Singapore, China. If an author were to attempt combining a love story of development practice and a scholarly text on digital transformation, this would be it."

—Luci Abrahams, *Director, LINK Centre, University of the Witwatersrand*

"Digital transformation, as Hanna amply demonstrates, is not just access to digital technology. It is a learning process by the whole society. The stories of Hanna's successes in various countries provide ample insights into digital transformation and its possibilities for development."

—Shinji Asanuma, *Visiting Professor, School of International and Public Policy, Hitotsubashi University*

"Nagy Hanna's book is another milestone in a large number of publications from a visionary leader. Sri Lanka benefited tremendously from Hanna's vision to create an integrated approach to take the dividends of ICT to every sector of our economy, despite a challenging implementation environment."

—Jayantha Fernando, *General Counsel, ICT Agency & Director, Sri Lanka CERT*

"I had the pleasure of working with Hanna for two decades. It would not be an exaggeration to say that Sri Lanka's ICT journey would not have come to fruition if Hanna did not champion this cause from the World Bank's side. His is a compelling story. Practitioners and students of development would find many nuggets of practical solutions to real life problems of implementation in a national setting fraught with language, cultural, social, and other polarities akin to most developing nations. Hanna's vision and heart are palpable throughout his story of digital transformation for inclusive development to which he has dedicated his life and poured his energy."

—Manju Haththotuwa, *Founding CEO, National ICT Agency and former CIO, Sri Lanka*

"Nagy Hanna exposes the challenges of making technology an effective tool for development, while confronting vested interests that seek to sustain the status quo, both in client governments and internally within the Bank. At the heart of the book is a powerful commitment to learning and using technology to change lives for the better."

—Tim Kelly, *Lead Digital Development Specialist, World Bank*

"What a life! This hugely engaging account of Hanna's career is motivated by his passionate commitment to development and belief in the potential of digital technologies to contribute to inclusive and sustainable development. His acute insights enable him to identify the many risks accompanying digital transformation and the barriers – institutional, political, cultural – to successful outcomes. He calls for holistic approaches to digital development. He emphasizes the crucial need for client buy-in and trust. He insists upon putting multi-stakeholder learning at the core of digital strategies."

—Robin Mansell, *Professor, London School of Economics and Political Science*

"Nagy Hanna has dedicated his career to digital development. He was a pioneer. He created the Bank's digital development community of practice - which mobilized expertise and funding to what was then an innovative new field. Hanna mentored and coached World Bank leadership and staff on technology for development."

—Samia Melhem, *Lead Digital Policy Specialist, World Bank*

"This inspiring book will benefit development practitioners and change agents across governments and development agencies."

—Mohamed Muhsin, *Former Vice President & CIO, World Bank*

"Drawing from his vast experience and pioneering role in the field, Hanna has woven together a remarkable story of his life and career. The book offers valuable lessons for policy makers and practitioners of digital technology. What Hanna conveys most convincingly is his early insight into the central role of digital technology in development. He illustrates this through examples from his firsthand experience. I had the good fortune to get to know him as a colleague at the World Bank where I witnessed his steadfast pursuit of his pioneering ideas in partnership with the country, and winning over critics. He practiced what he advocates in this book: nurturing local ownership and institutions, co-creating with stakeholders, prioritizing inclusion, and taking a holistic view. This book is a must-read for development professionals."

—Praful Patel, *Former Regional Vice President (Asia), World Bank*

"This book reflects the learning journey of a thought leader and pioneer in harnessing digital technology for development. Through detailed case studies, it ascribes top priority to digital development interventions in diverse country and regional contexts. Hanna's journey combines visionary thinking about digital transformation with hands-on lessons for translating country-driven visions into development programs and projects. He challenges development practitioners, policy makers, aid agencies, and developing countries to re-invent their practices to be fit for the digital age."

—Sam Pitroda, *former advisor to prime ministers of India*

"Nagy Hanna draws on his extensive experience in advising countries and the World Bank to point to the crucial task of developing the leadership, policies, institutions, competencies, partnerships, social learning and implementation mechanisms necessary to advance this transformation process. This candid text will be very useful for: policy makers who wish to integrate digital transformation and open government into national development strategies; business leaders wishing to transform their business or contribute to a growing digital industry; aid agencies' managers who want to accelerate their organizational learning and innovation; development practitioners who want to empower their clients with knowledge and resilience; and educators and students who want to understand the big picture and contribute to this transformative journey."

—Sanjay Pradhan, *CEO, Open Government Partnership and former VP, World Bank*

"The author had a distinguished career at the world's most visible international organization. He championed digital transformation and in virtue of his experience, he brings the reader to witness the fascinating evolution of development work across several decades. He describes the tumultuous change brought by technology at a crossroad of geopolitical, cultural and societal changes. In an exercise of retrospect (the author is a passionate art lover), the book reminds us of one of those Flemish paintings where the painter is in the picture, all devoted to provide the proportionate perspective to the external world."

—Carlo Rossotto, *Principal Investment Officer and Global Head, Upstream Telecom Media and Technology Infrastructure, International Finance Corporation*

"Hanna's pioneering study of information technology content of World Bank lending was a wakeup call for Bank leadership. His advocacy for Bank funding the study of India's opportunity for software export led to the exponential growth of India's software sector. I had the privilege of being a participant observer of Hanna's journey as a development economist to a passionate champion of digital transformation. This book shares the trials and triumphs of a developmental practitioner taking up this challenge. The development community needs more of his kind."

—Anil Srivastava, *President, Open Health Systems Lab and Founding Executive Director, NASSCOM*

"Nagy Hanna had to build the infrastructure within the World Bank and in Sri Lanka to realize the goal of digitally-enabled development. He helped us fashion the vision for e-Sri Lanka, build a new national ICT

Agency, get Bank financing and facilitate implementation of a pioneering digital transformation program. Hanna convinced the Bank, perhaps for the first time to provide operational funding to setup a brand-new agency and recruit right talent. He succeeded in creating an enabling environment and innovation funds for digital transformation. He persuaded the Bank to provide the necessary resources to innovate, learn and adapt through an evolving design, local ownership and political leadership. As a dedicated internationalist, Hanna ably argued the case of his client in the context of a difficult environment. A tightrope walk act between client and donor, which he balanced admirably. The book sums up the process and results. It lays out eloquently the trajectory of a pioneer—a gifted, committed and loyal development professional."

—Eran Wickramaratne, *MP, Founding Chairman ICT Agency & Former State Minister of Finance, Sri Lanka*

Contents

About the Author

Dr. Nagy K. Hanna is global expert on digital economy, national innovation, smart cities, and public and business digital transformation strategies. He is advisor, educator, author, and thought leader on digital policies, institutions, and strategies. He has 5 decades of experience in advising policymakers in developing policies and institutions in support of digital economy. He worked with public, private, and civil society leaders to promote digitally-enabled innovation and transformation in various economic sectors and geographic regions. He was the World Bank's first senior advisor on digital economy.

While a senior staff of the World Bank, spanning 30 years, he appraised and managed many World Bank-funded digital innovation, technical education, and institutional development/capacity-building programs. He was the lead corporate strategist of the World Bank. He pioneered the Bank's advisory services and lending for integrated digital transformation programs. He task managed World Bank assistance for India's first strategy for exporting software services. He founded and chaired a global forum on promoting digital innovation economies and building digital leadership institutions. He started his career with a focus on innovation and technology transfer, giving testimony to the United States House of Representatives on International Science and Technology Transfer Act.

He advises countries and aid agencies on developing institutions and leadership capabilities for integrating digital transformation programs into national development strategies. He was a visiting professor at Wits

University, South Africa, and a senior fellow and board member at the Center for Policy on Emerging Technologies. He co-founded People-Centered Internet, a global forum for inclusive Internet. He advised the US Government Office of Science and Technology on national competitiveness strategy. On the editorial boards of several journals on science, technology, and innovation, he published extensively on digital economy policies and institutions, and the role of government and aid agencies in the digital age. He holds advanced executive development degree from Harvard and PhD degree from University of Pennsylvania.

CHAPTER 1

Aims and Motivations

Abstract This chapter outlines the author's motivations to write a book on digital transformation informed by practice. The author reflects upon his motivations to write this book in light of the many challenges facing humanity today. He defines digital transformation as a process and ecosystem, and the role of digital foundations as core elements of this ecosystem. He argues for the role of digital transformation in pursuing inclusive and sustainable development.

Keywords Author's motivations · Defining digital transformation · Ecosystem · Digital foundations · Inclusive development

This book draws on my almost 50 years long journey as active participant-observer in economic development assistance in general and digital transformation practice, in particular. My aim is to offer emerging lessons learnt from practicing digital transformation by policymakers and development partners. Good practices are rapidly evolving to capture the opportunities opened by the digital revolution. Much can be learned from past technological revolutions and the sociopolitical and institutional adjustments that must be pursued to realize the potential substantial increases in productivity. Country leaders have to manage the risks and

N. K. Hanna, *Driving Digital Transformation in Developing Nations*, https://doi.org/10.1007/978-3-031-54573-3_1

unintended consequences that accompany revolutionary changes such as job losses, rising inequality, and cybersecurity.

The current and looming crises of climate change, growing inequality, dehumanizing poverty, unsustainable debts, and threats to democracy and governing must be matched by humankind capacity for adaptation, innovation, and learning. Fortunately, the revolutionary advances in digital technologies can help optimize the development and use natural and human resources to create smart cities, smart energy, smart infrastructure, smart finance, smart public services, and smart education and health, among others. This book aims at addressing the enabling policy and cultural environment necessary to invent both country-focused and global solutions for smart development.

Climate change is an overarching global challenge calling for a whole-of-government, whole-of-society, and whole-of-the-world approaches. The growing array of digital technologies may hold answers to this looming crisis through both adaptation and mitigation. The biggest impact digital technologies can have on climate change is to enable all, other economic sectors to reduce their greenhouse gas emission, by innovating new technologies that are more energy efficient. Digital technologies can also play a key role in strengthening the adaptive capacity of the country by supporting the processes of data gathering, decision-making, coordination, implementation, monitoring, and evaluation by all stakeholders and across the whole economy.

The rise of inequality and political polarization has been closely linked to the growth of digital platforms, social media-driven misinformation, and information monopolies. These trends feed on each other. Can the digital universe be socially governed to promote equity, mutual understanding, and peaceful coexistence? How can societies not fall prey to total digital business- and state-surveillance? How can digital services promote social and economic resilience, government transparency, and social empowerment?

Societies have to address novel equity and risk issues. Can governments catalyze digital technologies to ensure equitable access to public services and protect societies from associated risks? Can the governments, aid agencies, and business associations work with civil society organizations to strengthen governance, empower the marginalized, and make public services work for the poor?

This book aims to inform public policy in the digital age. It aims to empower development practitioners and reformers to improve digital development practice and realize its growing potential. Country experiences and those of development partners are examined to further develop the frameworks, tools, and processes that would advance both digital development theories and practices.

This book is an outcome of my "implementation research." It goes beyond the rhetoric and self-reporting of aid agencies, governments, and technology companies. The book focuses on the *processes* of digital diagnosis, strategy formulation, and strategy implementation, adaptation, evaluation, and learning. It shows how to maximize value from these processes.

Outcomes are shaped by the design of these processes. I seek to understand the interactions between government and local stakeholders, and between external advisors and local doers. I examine how diagnostic tools are applied and reshaped by the context and the user. The outcomes of these tools should help secure inclusive participation, build local ownership, and form coalitions for sustainable reform.

In this book, I share in-depth case studies of digital transformation of India, Sri Lanka, and other countries at government, city, sector, and regional levels. I draw on real-world examples of barriers to change that I and other practitioners encountered, and on ways of making progress in spite of them. I share how my ideas and conceptional frameworks of development have evolved through implementation research and co-learning with client countries.

My experience emphasizes the importance of integrating country development strategies (demand side—complements and capabilities) with technology strategies and applications (supply side—access to technology). I suggest ways to bring the two sides together as a transformation ecosystem. I draw on my comparative research to show that there are many lessons to be learned from the rich experiences of pioneering countries. No one-size fits all. This is a new field of development assistance with much to explore across countries at different levels of technology adoption and economic performance.

I also hope to help accelerate the learning curve of countries and aid agencies in leveraging digital transformation for development. Developing countries and aid agencies stand at an inflection point: disruptive technologies, primarily digital and data-driven, are creating new opportunities for growth, productivity, and inclusion. Given the pace of technological change, national governments, aid agencies, and new actors in development must accelerate their learning and develop effective collaboration strategies.

My most powerful motivation to write this book is my deep passion to help alleviate extreme poverty and suffering—a passion shaped by the personal experiences of my childhood and youth. Without passion for eliminating poverty and innovating solutions, I would not have endured the resistance and setbacks I faced working in a large and powerful but risk-averse bureaucracy. To me, writing this personal journey is an act of love: love for the impoverished and disempowered, for my fellow travelers who challenge aid agencies to fulfill their promise, and for country policymakers and reformers who face transformation challenges on the ground. It is also an act of hope that my experience will be of value to the younger generation of development practitioners.

Defining Digital Transformation

We can define digital transformation to mean using digital technologies to initiate and support deep and sustainable change in structures and processes, modes of production and consumption, value creation from available resources, and/or substantial increases in access to data. It is carried out at many levels, including organizations, economic sectors, government functions, cities, communities, and whole economies. Much of the use of digital technologies is done by individuals and for specific applications or services. Let us focus here on the restructuring of whole economies, where scale and impact of digital transformation are substantial and development assistance can be most influential. The country is my privileged entry point for development assistance.

Digital transformation is not just about user access to technology. It is a learning process by the whole society, especially if its full benefits were to be reaped and shared. That requires policy, institutional and ultimately cultural changes. It calls for a holistic approach to development that would help integrate the new technologies into development thinking and practice. It opens up development possibilities and accelerates organizational change and policy learning. Despite potentially superior payoffs from such integration, the case studies I share later demonstrate how incentives within aid agencies tend to reinforce a divide between development and technology policy specialists, and delay response to the imperatives of the digital age.

The ongoing digital revolution may be conceptualized in terms of sets of interrelated technologies that have come in two waves so far. An early wave brought the spread of computers, telecommunications reforms and privatization, reengineering government and business processes, development of databases, and introducing e-government and e-business applications. This wave may be dated to the late 1980s, and was reflected in the Bank's portfolio primarily in terms of computerization components of development projects. Much of the Bank's digital transformation assistance portfolio was driven by this wave.

This pace of technological change is unprecedented in the global history of technology. Its impact, however, is uneven, mainly due to the gap between the rapidly evolving technologies, on the one hand, and the lagging political and administrative institutions, on the other hand. The pace of digital change is forcing countries to update their development strategies to leverage digital innovations and new technologies. Effective adoption of these technologies by institutions and societies requires significant investment in skills and changes in mindset, roles, business processes, and working environments. It is important that all stakeholders have the incentives to make these investments.

Why Digital Transformation?

My research and work experience, and a fast-growing literature on innovation and economic transformation, convinced me that technological and institutional changes were fundamental to inclusive growth and poverty reduction. The rapid diffusion of digital technology and its impact on institutional change presented a unique opportunity for developing countries to accelerate economic transformation while promoting transparency, empowerment, and inclusion. I saw the Bank best positioned to leverage this general-purpose digital technology for shared prosperity at a global scale. Despite modest beginnings, I hoped to become a change agent to make it happen.

To be effective, development practitioners need to be able to learn from the past, as well as to imagine the future. Yet many consider the past obsolete and irrelevant in addressing technological change. My story suggests otherwise. Economic historians like to theorize about major changes in techno-economic paradigms of the past driven by general-purpose technologies (GPTs) and the profound economic and institutional upheavals that they caused.[1] Information technology is the GPT or the most disruptive technology of our time. It challenges development practices. Learning from past GPT disruptions is critical to translating digital technologies into economic competitiveness and shared prosperity today.

I learned to appreciate the various roles that digital technologies have been playing in transforming economic sectors and institutions, and more recently in capturing, processing, and sharing data and embedding intelligence into all kinds of infrastructures and services. They are crucial for sustainable development, in all contexts and at all stages of the development process (World Bank 2016; Hanna 1993, 2009; Gurin 2013). But the payoffs are not automatic or deterministic.

Artificial intelligence (AI) has rapidly emerged as a powerful new wave or set of tools for leveraging data and intelligence for global development. AI has been driven by rapidly increasing amount of accessible digital data, advances in machine learning algorithms, and more powerful processing power, and the expansion of broadband networks and digital platforms. For some forecasters, AI, combined with other widely diffused digital transformation tools, is expected to become the most powerful engine for prosperity in history.

But the risks and challenges AI will pose are becoming clear too. Development of AI remains heavily concentrated in a few advanced economies. AI is heavily dependent on the rest of digital transformation foundations, including enabling data sharing policies and advanced data science and innovation system. The emerging AI divide can also exacerbate inequality within societies. AI will likely create upheaval in the workforce. AI will no longer be limited to big tech companies.

Predictive AI uses patterns from the past to predict the future. In medicine, for example, predictive AI is already spreading in advanced countries, used for patient-centered treatment, augmenting diagnosis, and tailoring treatment. On the other hand, generative AI generates advanced content in response to prompts from users. It presents novel challenges. Together with social media, generative AI will make it tougher to tell facts from fiction. It can become a threat to democracy and free markets. It can be used for state and business surveillance. These challenges will

[1] General-purpose technologies (GPTs) are technologies that can affect an entire economy. GPTs have the potential to drastically alter societies through their impact on pre-existing economic and social structures. See, for example, Carlota Perez (2002).

demand both local and global responses. Like any tool, both types of AI must be studied rigorously and deployed carefully. They must be added to the digital transformation ecosystem.

My advocacy for digital transformation should be put in perspective. Data, knowledge, and communication are present in one form or another in any development process. The digital revolution is impacting almost all forms of production, consumption, learning, and social life. Yet, digital transformation is not the sole solution for everything or can be treated as such in isolation. It is a profound, technologically driven force for change. It must be complemented by other socio-technical changes and adapted to local contexts to produce smart solutions to global and local challenges. It must be complemented by relevant policies, institutions, skills, and new ways of doing business to produce the desired outcomes.

Despite versatility and universality of digital technologies, country context matters. For the fragile and low-income countries, digital technologies hold much promise of substantial increases in productivity, resilience, public services, and technological leapfrogging. But they also bring to countries novel risks and vulnerabilities such as digital exclusion, surveillance, monopolies, misinformation, and costly unrealized benefits. The roles of ICT multinationals and aid agencies vary accordingly. For middle-income countries, the digital sector offers major opportunities for quality jobs, exports, and enhanced services and quality of life. Socio-economic context and country development priorities must shape and give directions to digital transformation.

Progressively, I shifted my perspective from focusing on ICT components of development projects or silos of sectoral applications to economy-wide deployment of digital technologies and building the ecosystems of digital transformation for whole economies (Fig. 1.1). The foundations part of the ecosystem included the digital policies, institutions, capabilities, culture, and data and communications infrastructure. These foundations were not only necessary to secure the expected payoffs from growing investments in digital technology applications. They were essential to enable diverse innovations at the grassroots and national levels, led by government, business, and civil society. They are still growing as part of the transformation ecosystem, and in response to new digital technology innovations and capabilities.

This shift was informed by the experience of pioneering nations like Singapore. But it was not an easy shift to treat digital development as a strategic and cross-cutting dimension of development since this shift

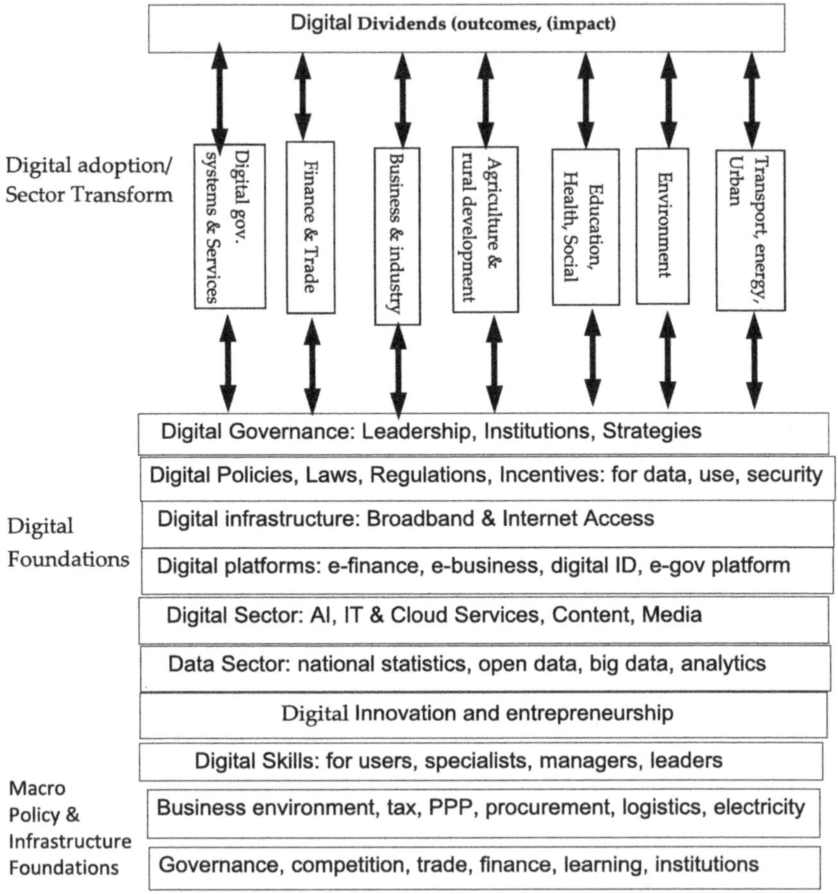

Fig. 1.1 Digital transformation ecosystem (Hanna 2020)

would threaten the status quo of aid bureaucracies and sector silos, as demonstrated in the chapters on India and Sri Lanka.

Working with digital pioneers like Singapore and India during the 1990s, I observed the transformational power of digital technologies and felt very strongly that developing countries could not afford to miss out on harnessing these powerful technologies for sustainable development and poverty alleviation. Helping countries to leapfrog to the digital economy became the leitmotif of my work, sometimes exhilarating, at other times heartbreaking, but always worth the effort. Over the years, the intrinsic rewards of fulfilling my calling while working on innovative and learning-intensive tasks would usually outweigh the frustration of coping with a risk-averse bureaucracy.

Digital transformation can provide an opportunity to get the country's elite to strike a "development bargain" (Dercon 2022). Political leaders can be attracted to having their countries participate in the digital revolution both as suppliers and users of digital solutions. I experienced this first-hand in my discussions with leaders in the public, private, and civil society sectors. The digital revolution raises new aspirations and possibilities to leapfrog, modernize, and accelerate the economic development process. It is an opportunity to help build an attractive vision of development for both the elites and society at large.

CHAPTER 2

Developing India's First Transformation Strategy

Abstract This chapter covers an in-depth case study of Bank-client collaborative practice. The Bank financed a study of India's software export strategy when the industry was still in its infancy in 1990. The demonstrated impact of this technical assistance suggests lessons for collaborative and catalytic roles for aid agencies. Building on this breakthrough, I worked with local stakeholders on a proposal for the Bank to finance a comprehensive strategy and investment program for integrating ICT into India's development strategy. The Bank refused to finance it on the grounds that India was not ready for such a "high-tech" strategy. A missed opportunity for forming an enduring partnership on digital development between the Bank and a pioneering country.

Keyword Bank-client collaboration · India · Software industry · Export strategy · Country development strategy

India is where I first began to understand the role of information technology in development. I first visited there as a tourist, guided by a book on the brief cultural history of India. With my wife's help in art history and travel planning, I grew to appreciate India's long and rich art history. We did not travel under the protection of guided tourist groups or official

N. K. Hanna, *Driving Digital Transformation in Developing Nations*,
https://doi.org/10.1007/978-3-031-54573-3_2

Bank missions, so I saw not only the political and technological sophistication of business and political leaders but also the extreme poverty of millions. I experienced a country of immense diversity and contrasts.

India has been a major laboratory for development assistance by the Bank and other development partners, I was also inspired by the talented Indian business leaders and entrepreneurs in India and Silicon Valley, so I wanted to engage with India as soon as I could to partner in the promising field of digital technology and software services. Could India show the way for accelerated, inclusive, and sustainable development in a 1.3 billion strong democracy?

Spurring India's Software Services

In 1990, I was invited to join the Asia Technical Department of the Bank. The department was headed by Dan Ritchie, who expressed interest in my early work on the *Information Technology Revolution and Economic Development (Hanna 1990, 1991)*. I was expected to lead the department's work on digital technology, covering East and South Asia regions. I was willing to accept a downgrade in rank and move to the technical department to allow me to pioneer this work in the Asia Region.

The department was created during a major World Bank reorganization in 1987. It was expected to provide a critical mass of expertise in areas that could not be covered at the country level. Country directors were incentivized to fund their own staff, they would seek support from the technical department only as a last resort. This meant the technical department would act as a pool of internal consultants to the country level that monopolized the client relationship. This arrangement discouraged the evolution of new creative areas of development assistance as well as the engagement of expertise in technology and innovation. Ultimately, this led to the abolition of regional technical departments, but at the time, I was not aware of any of these issues.

I started with overseeing the implementation of a recently approved Electronics Industry Development project. It was a "one of a kind" project in a promising industry that India was keen to promote by emulating the successes of several East Asian countries. The focus was on hardware, a carry-over from the 1970s to 1980s electronics buzz. The project involved a Bank loan of about US$ 250 million to support a line of credit for investing in electronics manufacturing, engineering education, and technical assistance for research and training. A small one million dollar component was allocated to support the development of a national strategy for the software services industry.

This component buried in the $250 million Bank loan was too small to attract Bank management attention. As is typically the case in technical assistance, the study was done at the request of the government, driven by two entrepreneurial Bank staff, Rob Schware and myself, and by a few key leaders and founders of the National Association of Software Services Companies (NASSCOM), including Harish Mehta, Dewang Mehta, Narayana Murthy, Nandan Nilekani, Ashank Desai, Anil Srivastava, and Saurabh Srivastava.

These mavericks were also complemented or enabled by few reformers in the public service who listen to the needs of the nascent industry, as advocated by NASSCOM, and helped to remove the antiquated policies and bureaucratic constraints to the young industry. On the Bank side, credit also goes to Geoff Gowen who was the initial task manager. The study was expected to lead to a staff report for both the Government and the Bank. Rob Schware was a maverick and one of the few Bank staff with knowledge of the software services industries. The private sector (NASSCOM), public sector (public policy reformers), and the World Bank (intrapreneurs, development financiers) created a triangle that complemented and reinforced each other in pursuit of a common goal: to advocate and create a vibrant ecosystem for the nascent but promising industry.

NASSCOM thought the Bank really cared about this small technical assistance component (report), but in fact, Bank management was unaware of the importance of this nascent sector, and Bank staff had to keep their "skunk work" invisible. Early visibility of the study would have led to Bank management take-over and undermined NASSCOM's report ownership and advocacy in India and abroad. Moreover, at the time, the Bank swore by market fundamentalism: it was against industrial policy and "picking winners."

As the task team leader for the multi-component Electronics project, I devoted most of the implementation assistance resources to creating and disseminating the strategy and subsequently to developing a more comprehensive Digital India strategy. The study was carried out by a global consulting firm and was based on intensive consultations with NASSCOM and several government departments. The Bank team was aware it did not have in-depth expertise in the software industry and so acted as catalyst and facilitator, letting NASSCOM take the lead. The

Bank's brand helped to strengthen the voice of the nascent Association in advocating policy reforms to promote India's software services abroad. It acted as a convener of all key stakeholders, cutting across the government and private sectors.

In retrospect, timing for Bank engagement was critical to capture a window of opportunity when the global demand for software services was growing exponentially. Advances in data telecommunications enabled outsourcing, and India's skilled manpower was available at competitive rate. Then, NASCOM was a small and anxious to get external help to influence government policies and promote exports in services. The Bank's timely engagement could make a difference, even though the opportunity was not obvious to the Bank's senior management.

We, Bank staff, acted as "hand-holders" rather than "taskmasters." Perhaps we acted as entrepreneurs, inspired by our country counterparts who were the true entrepreneurs, reformers, and change agents. Client relationship was informal, based on trust, openness, and flexibility. Bank staff did not have the benefit or constraint of a blueprint. They were working on the frontier of the Bank's global knowledge, driven by vision, commitment, and excitement about a new field of development. They secured ownership and partnership with key stakeholders. In this case, the Bank leveraged its reach and access to policymakers and its credibility as an honest broker. The final report and its findings were widely presented in India, the Silicon Valley, and major US cities. NASSCOM remained in the driver's seat at these presentations. This helped change perceptions and built a broad base of support for subsequent policy reforms.

The software export study aimed to estimate the size of the global market for software services, and the niches that India could fill. Much of the data had to be constructed, as they were not publicly available then. This provided a vision for "stretch" targets for India's software exporters. It aimed to raise India's IT exports from $130 million in 1990 to one billion in five years—then was an ambitious target. It outlined the main policy reforms needed to facilitate the exports of these services and the initiatives required to develop more value-added services. It also identified the initial opportunities open to Indian and foreign investors to capitalize on India's comparative and competitive advantages. It provided a strong signal to policymakers, private investors, and entrepreneurs.

Learning from a Success Story

One clear indicator of success is annual export revenue of Indian software and services. In 1990 it was estimated at US$ 130 million. By 2022, it grew to US$ 193 billion—far exceeding expectations.

Success has many fathers. Credit goes to key NASSCOM contributors and India's entrepreneurs. Since the 1990s, India's ICT industry was driven by a set of highly motivated entrepreneurs. Narayana Murthy, one of NASSCOM founders and chairman of Infosys, invested substantial time and funds. Tata Consulting Services (TCS) and Tata Infotech were also major contributors. But the Association was lean and not financially self-supporting. Members acted cohesively as a "coalition of competitors."[1]

The Association identified key policy issues that hampered the growth of the member companies and engaged in lobbying with concerned government departments and policymakers to ease those constraints. Telecom (bandwidth) was a major issue, with a government-owned monopoly for overseas communications. Another issue was the 110% software import duty at a time when allowing duty-free imports would provide opportunities for training and help build India's competitive advantage in software services. Another issue was the availability of finance, particularly venture capital and foreign exchange. NASSCOM was instrumental in solving some of these major challenges in partnership with a few reformers in the government.

NASSCOM played policy education, agenda-setting, and advocacy roles. It promoted IT as a sunrise sector and made it synonymous with "India's tomorrow." In lobbying, it did not advocate protectionist policies for the software industry: it encouraged openness in importing software and in welcoming foreign IT firms who could help position India as an IT hub. It adopted the populist slogan of "bandwidth" as an essential requirement for software exports and social well-being which became a catalyst for the telecom reforms in the 1990s. It created awareness of the high value of software and encouraged government policies to pay for this "intangible," unbundled from the hardware: paying for software required a major change in the customer mindset. NASSCOM also encouraged the shift from body shopping (IT services specialists working on-site)

[1] See Kiran Karnik (2012), *The Coalition of Competitors*, for excellent history of India's IT industry.

to working in India (offshore), to the development of generic software products and business process outsourcing and IT-enabled services. These transitions were not automatic and required new business models and innovations that were informed by the increasing understanding of the businesses of their overseas partners. The Indian diaspora in the USA acted as a bridge.

An increasing number of India's policymakers and government bureaucrats evolved the policies and procedures to liberate the ICT sector from the stranglehold of old policies and archaic procedures. In some cases, they went further and developed proactive policies, such as software technology parks that provided reliable bandwidth for global connectivity at low cost, together with shared support services and tax incentives for exports. These parks attracted many large and small software enterprises, including foreign investors. The Department of Electronics (DoE) subsequently allowed software companies to set up anywhere in India and still enjoy tax incentives. The DoE facilitated the establishment of the National Informatics Center (NIC), the Computer Maintenance Corporation (CMC), and the National Software Technology (NCST), among other centers of expertise. These institutions played a critical role in creating software talent capabilities and spurring the development of IT applications, particularly to suit government needs.

In short, the long-term commitment of the government encouraged the private sector and enabled the IT industry to plan and invest for the long term. The government offered a helping hand to a new breed of entrepreneurs who were not dependent on government subsidies or bribes. In 1999, the Minister of Finance chaired a high-level task force that created a more industry-friendly policy environment. Recognizing the growth potential of the industry, Indian states competed to attract IT investment. Senior bureaucrats of these states even traveled abroad to speak at industry forums to promote India's capabilities in this sector.

I listened to India's software entrepreneurs and learned about the needs of their young industries and enterprises. The emerging class of entrepreneurs and young engineers was inspiring. The software industry presented a clear opportunity as starting a business in this sector mainly required intellectual (seed or sweat capital) rather than financial capital. There were no major business conglomerates or public monopolies in the sector. The industry required far fewer licenses, clearances, and transactions with government departments. Entry and exit barriers were low. These tech-entrepreneurs helped create a magic culture similar to Silicon

Valley—a culture that linked export markets, global IT corporate users, and global best practices.

I also engaged in dialogue with Department of Electronics' secretary Roy Paul, Telecom Ministry's secretary Vittal, the chairman of ICICI Vagul, and the CEO of Tata Consulting Services (TCS), F.C. Kohli to further advance these causes. Unfortunately, these sector-specific issues were not on the Bank's development agenda for India, as the Bank was then preoccupied with India's balance of payment problem and other macro policy issues. I incorporated some of the challenging issues into a Bank funding proposal to support an e-India strategy and hoped such a major free-standing ICT project would provide a better platform for sector-wide policy reforms (more later).

The Bank played a catalyzing role, working both with the young association, NASSCOM, and with reformers within the Indian government. It was already involved in a large investment portfolio of ICT components in development projects, so it had some credibility in harnessing ICT for development, particularly in public sector projects. India's software industry was facing many challenges, and the young association needed an independent and credible voice to add to its own in dealing with the government a time when government regulations were stifling, and some government technocrats were just preparing for reform. The government was ready to make an exception for urgently needed reforms in a promising sector with few large public ICT enterprises. Bank assistance, however modest in terms of dollars, was responsive and timely. It was an early milestone in India's ICT industry journey. It helped the government and other stakeholders realize the potential of the ICT industry, and the need to engage with key industry players and other stakeholders. The study also provided visibility for India's technological skills and quality in the global markets far beyond the ICT sector. It led to many unanticipated impacts.

The interplay among business actors (NASSCOM, digital entrepreneurs, CEOs of consulting and software firms), senior public servants (policymakers in ministries of electronics, telecommunications, and trade), and World Bank (few frontline development professionals) constituted a triangle that drove the nascent industry forward. Each group or corners of the triangle faced many challenges within their sectors or organizations. Their collaboration complemented each other's resources and pushed for reforms in an environment that was not hospitable for innovation or partnership. The private sector, represented by NASSCOM leadership, was perhaps the most critical partner and driver. This is not surprising in view of dynamism and promise of a fast-growing and evolving local digital industry.

The success of the software services industry had many spillovers and wider impacts on India's economy. The strong demand for software skills gave rise to a related industry segment: the ICT education and training sector. At the start of India's software exports drive, there were fears that India would quickly lose its pool of skilled manpower to opportunities at MNCs. Industry leaders emphasized the need for massive investment in ICT training. State governments and the private sector responded by opening several private engineering colleges and strengthening engineering education in public universities and IITs. The growing demand made professional education in this area an attractive investment. Some large software consulting firms, particularly TCS, invested heavily in ICT training, beyond their internal needs, both to cushion against the relatively high attrition of scarce ICT talent, and as an attractive business on its own. A thriving new industry of professional education took root and a whole new training industry was created. Capitalizing on the strong demand for ICT services, private training institutes aimed at making science and math graduates employable in the ICT sector.

The Indian ICT industry changed the global perception of Indian quality. Many Indian software companies invested in achieving the highest quality standards. The quality perception of India's IT services has undergone a sea of change. By the late 1990s, India has established itself as a destination for low-cost/high-quality talent beyond software exports.

Leveraging Software for Development?

In the early 1990s, the potential contribution of the ICT sector to India's economic development was negligible. ICT sectoral penetration in industry, finance, at all levels of government and among public sector banks, was slow. In 1990, national spending on computer hardware and software was estimated at 0.4% of GDP compared to 0.8% in Korea, 1.1% in Ireland, 1.3% in Singapore, and 1.4% in Israel. Most OECD countries spent between 3 and 5% of their GDP on IT. India's ICT sector was also much smaller than that of other Asian countries. NASSCOM was too busy with lucrative foreign markets to attend to India's underdeveloped domestic market.

What factors contributed to this imbalance? Why was India lagging in leveraging its substantial software capabilities for the benefit of the whole economy? Many countries insist that ICT companies roll-out their solutions domestically before they can sell them abroad. The successful computerization of India's Railways' passenger reservation system in 1987 was one such example. In addition to its wide socio-economic impact in India, it led to a key role in computerizing London's subway system. A developing domestic software market can prevent an over-reliance on the ups and downs of the main export market.

There were other factors that constrained domestic learning, with major implications for the whole economy. National policies then favored local hardware manufacturers. Data communications infrastructure and private support services were underdeveloped. Indian hardware and software suppliers invested little in user education and domestic marketing. Public procurement and information management practices were poor. IT professionals lacked business orientation. Trade policies across sectors were protectionist, which weakened incentives for IT adoption and investment in IT user skills. Links between local IT suppliers and users were weak as users were not organized to share experiences, learn from suppliers, and demand quality and fair play. MNCs were major beneficiaries of large government IT programs and aided projects. Local capabilities in systems integration and change management were scarce and domestic IT users were unwilling to pay for intangible services such as technical assistance and complementary consulting services. There were also fears of jobs loss and skills obsolescence. These and other factors impeded local ICT adoption and digital transformation dividends across the economy.[2]

Taking a broad view of India's digital transformation would have led to revealing human resources constraints to domestic digital adoption and learning—a glaring contrast between highly advanced research and digital skills in the digital sector, and less developed primary and secondary education to ensure inclusive digital literacy. Unfortunately, India's Ministry of Education and the Bank's Educational Department were not ready to pursue the educational reforms necessary for an inclusive digital economy. Aspirations were limited to developing and mobilizing the technical skills needed for software export services. Taking

[2] Some of these issues were identified in a UNDP-sponsored seminar in 1991: "Software: an engineering industry, need for developing a domestic market."

an inclusive national ICT ecosystem view would have been helpful in attending to this domestic user capability gap and thus advancing a holistic IT strategy.

Working with NASSCOM and key policymakers and reformers in government, I wanted to engage the Bank in partnering with India to develop and finance a comprehensive IT strategy that would support India's development strategy. The IT strategy would address the opportunities and constraints facing the sector and help create a shared vision to leverage ICT for inclusive socio-economic development (Hanna 1994). I was particularly interested in addressing the underdeveloped domestic market, where most of the potential ICT benefits lie without reinforcing India's high level of income inequality. Why was demand for ICT adoption lagging behind the need and potential? I felt the timing was right for engaging the Bank in constructive dialogue with local actors on major policy reforms and long-term investment in digital infrastructure and applications development programs. There was a window of opportunity for a potential shift in the policy environment. ICT was viewed as "India's tomorrow."

I conducted a study that outlined the rationale for a coherent long-term ICT strategy to enhance India's competitiveness while promoting inclusive development (Hanna 1994). The main elements were: (1) measures to mobilize demand in the local private sector (SMEs) and to target investments in strategic applications for the public sector and financial modernization; (2) programs to strengthen software industry capabilities and export networks; and (3) policy and infrastructure (data communication, skills) measures to strengthen both supply and demand for software and ICT services and lay the foundations for sustained development. The study outlined some broad and complementary roles for government: to create competitive markets for ICT; and to improve investment and use of ICT in public administration and service delivery. The government—in collaboration with private sector institutions—would also develop incentives, extension services, data policies, and other market-enhancing mechanisms to address specific market failures in the supply and diffusion of ICT. These would target small software firms and user enterprises.

I drafted a Project Concept Note for a proposed project that was formally endorsed by the heads of three ministries/departments: Electronics (DOE), Telecom, and Economic Affairs (DEA). A long-awaited meeting on the concept note was chaired by the country director for

India. My prospects of pursuing such exciting but risky projects hung in the balance. The note drew on broad local consultations and substantial knowledge I have accumulated. It also conveyed stakeholder enthusiasm about Bank support of the emerging sunrise sector.

The decision meeting was chaired by the country director (CD) who made up his mind before the meeting even started. Despite the large audience gathered for the meeting, he declared at the outset he only had a few minutes to spare. Without asking for the views of participants from across the Bank, he immediately announced he could not approve such a project for several reasons: Indian decision-makers do not use information in their management; India lacks reliable electricity to enable software export services, and IT is a high-tech sector that is not relevant to poverty reduction in India! He left before a discussion could unfold. In a subsequent meeting with the division chief, I proposed a scaled-down pilot, but was told that the planned lending program for India was large in terms of dollars but limited in terms of lending operations, so there was no room for small innovative projects—what he called "boutique operations." It was much easier for the Bank to transfer a billion dollars through a Structural Adjustment Loan (SAL) or Balance of Payment operation, in a single transaction, than approve a $50 million investment project that required innovation, local adaptation, and hands-on implementation assistance.

I could not challenge the Country Director's (CD) dismal view of India and the ICT sector in general. And there was no place in the Bank to challenge a CD decision to kill a client-owned project or to hold him accountable for a missed opportunity to help the client.

With my immediate management support, I drafted a paper that proposed an ICT development and diffusion strategy for India. It presented the issues involved in formulating a national strategy. The paper took account of emerging international experience and applied it to India's socio-economic conditions. The foreword stated that "the paper is neither a blueprint plan nor a formal or informal Bank proposal. Any detailed blueprint for a national information technology plan should emerge from extensive discussion and consultation between the public and private sectors in India." The paper only described a vision and an approach to formulating a strategy. It outlined the strategic elements of a national strategy that could be further developed through the collaborative efforts of public and private sector leaders.

In view of the above setbacks and obstacles, I proposed to my Indian counterparts to hold a national conference to air the issues and options raised by the paper, and engage MNC leaders (such as Microsoft and Apple), ICICI (private bank), NASSCOM founders, chief executives of progressive Indian states (like AP), the Prime Minister's office, etc. The aim was to use this forum to develop a shared national vision and build coalitions for reform. It was important to develop a national consensus on the broad outlines of a strategy to mobilize the support of interested aid agencies. We did an extensive search for possible speakers and panelists; government invitations were sent to many local and international thought leaders. Nevertheless, the country director blocked the event—probably fearing it would add to the pressure on him to reverse his decision to prohibit Bank engagement in the sector.

I wish we learned more from those change leaders and entrepreneurs. The Bank could have mobilized them to share their experiences throughout the Asia region and beyond. It was a missed opportunity to learn with a major transforming country! More broadly, a missed opportunity to provide intellectual leadership and a platform for best practice sharing for the benefit of low- and middle-income countries.

Innovating with a Leading Client

India has created innovative programs for applying digital technologies in the public, private, and civil society sectors. For decades, the Bank has been funding IT components in various sectoral projects and programs, but remained inwardly focused, unwilling to experiment and innovate and incapable of a strategic partnership in support of the country's national development strategy.

Many factors worked in India's favor for harnessing digital technology for development. *First of all*, it had *champions at the political level*. Andhra Pradesh (AP) Chief Minister Chandrababu Naidu and Prime Minister Rajiv Gandhi promoted government computerization, and Advani as the Deputy PM pushed the national e-Governance agenda. Minister Pitroda served as chairman of the National Knowledge Commission (2005–2009), a high-level advisory body to the Prime Minister of India, to offer policy recommendations for improving knowledge-related institutions and infrastructure in the country. The National Knowledge Commission submitted around 300 recommendations on 27 focus areas. I had the opportunity to engage with these leaders, mainly outside the Bank. They would have preferred a more enduring knowledge partnership and a more comprehensive policy dialogue with the Bank going beyond Bank procurement and project-specific technical issues.

Secondly, Technocrats in Government. Bureaucrats were gradually being turned into or replaced by technocrats. The selective national civil service established programs for public sector Chief Information Officers and raised a new breed of civil service officers educated in computer sciences. They led multiple innovations in their ministries and departments. Secretaries or senior officers Chandrashekhar and Satya Narayana were among them.

Thirdly, Innovators in NGOs and Corporations. E-Choupal is an example of an imaginative ICT initiative started in India by the ITC corporation. This system provides farmers with weather, good farming practices, and crop market price information and allows to sell crops directly to buyers through its network. Many social entrepreneurs have created innovative solutions to lower the cost of access to the Internet and share local knowledge and content online for the benefit of rural India. Pilots were everywhere but scaling "grassroots innovation" to meet the enormous needs of the poor remained a challenge.

ICT specialists at the Bank were closely involved in many of India's ICT initiatives through key components of Bank-funded projects in various sectors. But the Bank remained largely reactive, short-term oriented, inwardly focused, and risk-averse. Its ICT assistance was ad-hoc, on a project-by-project basis, and it did not aim to capture the opportunities and address the threats of the environment, or respond to the special needs of the client. Assistance was limited by the Bank's own weaknesses in the ICT field and often relied on the TTLs' call upon the few technically skilled staff available in the Bank's central digital development unit.

The Bank engaged in several pilots using *InfoDev*—a multi-donor trust fund where the Bank acted as the executing agency. One example was a healthcare project to deliver quality health services to the rural population of Andhra Pradesh (AP). Another was to operationalize a grassroots innovations augmentation network (GIAN) and a Knowledge Network (KN) of grassroots innovators. The KN attempted to establish an experimental wide area network of farmers, rural extension workers, and researchers in agricultural institutions in the state of Gujarat to share results in field experiments, new tools, and other innovations. A third was to create India's development information network, and so on. These were proof-of-concept pilots prior to scaling. The challenge of scaling was common at that time, and India was sometimes called "the country with a million startups." But the pilots were still valuable in providing timely technical assistance and bottom-up innovations for priority target groups.

In addition to the *InfoDev*-funded projects, the Government of India fully supported the Bank's Development Gateway—another donor-funded program. The India portion of the development gateway included the establishment of the India Country Gateway and a Research and Training Center (R&T) for the DGF. The India Country Gateway's objective was to facilitate the use of new ICT technologies in the health, education, agriculture, and other development sectors.

Several e-readiness assessment reports were funded by the *InfoDev* and Development Gateway trust funds and carried out during the early 2000s. They were shared at the highest levels of government. The poor state of readiness at both central and state levels created a sense of urgency within the government. These reports became the foundation of India's National e-Government Plan (NeGP).

The take away: technical assistance can have high payoffs when it is based on mutual trust, even without major Bank funding. In fact, many of these innovative pilots relied on trust funds which allowed task managers ample room to capture opportunities and outsource expertise, without much Bank bureaucracy. Yet, the Bank lost the opportunity to build a cumulative learning process and a long-term partnership due to frequent staff changes and a lack of agreement on Bank assistance priorities in this dynamic area. In the early 2000s, India moved toward developing major programs for digital government, universal digital identity, smart cities, and many others. More often than not, the bank has not been the partner of choice to support these programs.

How Can the Bank Raise Its Game?

The Bank was requested to assist in ambitious and complex programs totaling billions of dollars. ICT staff provided significant analytical inputs to the development of the digital government and smart city programs. But the Bank was running behind in its technical capabilities vis-a-vis its major client. For example, the Indian government and the Bank agreed on a 15-year funding program for the National e-Governance Plan (NeGP) and approved the first 5-year project, but due to various procurement and administrative disagreements, the Bank was only able to approve a development policy loan for $150 million of the $5.5 billion program.

In order to address the growing concerns within the government, India's Planning Commission and ICT Ministry launched its "Guidelines for Capacity Building and Institutional Framework for e-Governance" under the National e-Governance Plan (NeGP). The NeGP was formulated by the Department of Information Technology (DIT) and the Department of Administrative Reforms & Public Grievances. In 2006, the Union Government approved NeGP's capacity-building guidelines.

The Government of India (GoI) realized the need for a holistic view of the several e-Governance initiatives implemented across the country. To accelerate e-Governance across the various arms and levels of government a program approach guided by a common vision and strategy was necessary. A national program would have the added advantage of enabling savings in costs by sharing the core and support infrastructure, enforcing interoperability through standards, resulting in a seamless customer experience.

The Bank team worked with the Ministry's team on the NeGP, and in parallel, a Bank loan for $300 million (e-Bharat Project) was prepared to support the NeGP program nationally. The e-Bharat investment loan was approved by the Bank at the Regional VP level and was ready to go. However, there were serious disagreements about the Bank's procurement requirements and institutional arrangements. The Bank's procurement officers did not support India's framework contracts for ICT procurement. In a VP-chaired Bank review meeting, I argued for investing in a portion of the program and adopting gradual and mutually agreed on improvements over time, rather than fencing off Bank-funded projects with different procurement and institutional arrangements. The government backed out of the Bank's proposed institutional framework conditions for creating an independent authority for the NeGP national program.

In response to the GOI decision, the Bank's project team prepared two sets of projects: the e-Bharat Project (an investment lending for US$ 300 million) and, the India E-Services Development Policy Loan (US$150 million) to support the total cost of the whole program of $5.5 billion. In the end, the US$300 million Investment Loan and the proposed program approach to support NeGP were put on hold. The Bank's support was restricted to the US$150 million Development Policy Loan meant to address program policy and ecosystem.

Did the Development Policy Loan make any difference to the e-government plan or execution? The Bank-funded preparation of both proposed projects made a significant impact on India's e-Government initiative, regardless of the actual size of loans. It provided the foundation for a much larger initiative over the years. In 2014, NeGP was renamed as e-Kranti (or e-revolution) and became one of the key components of Digital India. The Project Development Fund and the Program Management Unit (PMU) were created under the Bank-funded Project and were renamed "Digital India Corporation."

Was the Bank too rigid in its procurement approach? The Bank's procurement approach was the main reason why the e-Bharat investment loan stalled. The Bank required applying Bank Procurement Rules to the "entire national program" valued at $5.5 billion, even while proposing to finance a small share of the ambitious program. The Ministry of Electronic and Information Technology (MeitY) did not agree—as it was not feasible to manage over 200 projects implemented by various ministries and state governments across the country in line with Bank rules. The other issue was MeitY's innovative "Framework Contracts" approach where it had agreed with ICT vendors on fixed rates based on pre-defined technical specifications. The Bank insisted on bidding for every sub-project.

What lessons can be learned from Bank-country collaboration on the national e-Governance program? This was a major experience where the Bank was a co-learner with an advanced client. For Bank staff, learning was limited to a few individuals who since left their jobs. With continuing Bank staff turnover, it is unlikely that this learning has been retained or institutionalized.

The Bank tried to impose its procedures on an ambitious, complex, and innovative national program for the digital transformation of many state governments. India demonstrated that the Bank's "one size fits all" approach, irrespective of the client's needs and capabilities, is a stifling bottleneck to effective collaboration. At that time, the Bank lacked flexible policy lending instruments. Rigid procurement and other fiduciary requirements had to be adapted and updated. The Bank needed to develop systems to monitor the entire project life cycle, since opportunities for corruption do not occur only at the procurement stage, but whenever the contractor payments are made. The Bank also needed to build innovative digital M&E Systems—to monitor outputs and results. Bank rules were too 'Project Inputs driven'—focusing on procurement, funds, hiring, etc. This experience suggested the Bank should become more open to taking on risks associated with maximizing development outcomes and learning.

Deliberate country assistance strategy, partnership with local stakeholders, in-depth country knowledge, and shared vision and learning were all necessary for such long-term programs. More dedicated client-focused ICT teams were needed to fully understand the challenges and priorities of a complex country like India. Economy-wide ICT assistance strategies for major clients like India are a must, but cannot be prepared remotely from Washington's digital development global practice unit.

The Bank-country director for India played a proactive role in making digital applications support a part of the director's consistent funding mandate and subject to a professional review by an ICT specialist. India represented a major country with a large ICT portfolio to have a dedicated ICT specialist work across all sectors. The specialist was locally placed and funded as part of the country management unit and enjoyed some continuity across time and sectors. After an initial hesitancy to fund an integrated free-standing e-India, the Bank increasingly engaged in integrating digital transformation components into regular development programs. The quality of assistance and integration of these components into sectoral programs depended largely on the quality of cooperation between TTLs and resident ICT experts. Implementation was facilitated by ample local skills available for systems integration, platform development, and digital transformation. When cooperation was secured, ICT components in sector projects won national awards for innovation and best practices.[3]

Looking ahead, India and the Bank can benefit from mutual learning and share best practices with other leading countries. India needs to further adapt its digital transformation strategy to new opportunities and threats: rising Asia and China, globalization, demographic pressures, rising inequality, new competitive centers for outsourcing, shifts in global markets for ICT services, etc. Export growth is likely to come from new markets, new customers, and value-added knowledge services. Domain knowledge and innovation will increasingly become key to high-value IT jobs. Indian universities will need to partner with the public and private sectors to create development-focused solutions and train a twenty-first-century skilled workforce. Cybersecurity will rise in importance. Competition in ICT services will come from fast followers of middle-income countries.

[3] https://ehealth.eletsonline.com/2009/12/tamil-nadu-health-systems-project-successful-implementation-of-hmis-across-government-hospitals/.

India's domestic market remains untapped. The public sector should not fall further behind business practices, as it provides basic services for the entire population and creates the policy environment for all stakeholders to join the knowledge economy. ICT offers opportunities to fight corruption and practice open government. Massive and rapid urbanization drives the need to integrate environmentally sustainable smart city solutions with equitable access to basic urban services. India's unique identity (UID) has become a platform for Public–Private Partnerships (PPPs) and the delivery of services for all citizens. India's private domestic market offers substantial opportunities for the growth of a healthy and robust ICT services industry. Call centers and Business Process Offshoring (BPO) to serve domestic clients are increasingly in demand by the private sector. Many Indian ICT companies have yet to explore the domestic market, particularly for meeting the needs of SMEs.

Did the Bank "miss the boat" by not partnering with India on its fast-evolving digital agenda early on, when it could have had maximum impact on policy and strategy? As of this writing (2022), there is no explicit future-oriented and mutually agreed-upon digital development strategy for Bank engagement in India at the national and sub-national levels. The Bank could have leveraged its early (1990–91) partnership with NASSCOM that focused on software exports and could have helped reorient local software capabilities to serve the domestic market and public services. It could have catalyzed best practices diffusion across its substantial investment portfolio in India. A partnership could have also helped spread India's socio-technical innovations to other poor regions and countries.

My own partnership with Indian colleagues and my advocacy for digital India started around 1990 and outlasted my Bank career that ended in 2005. I moved from being an observer of India's first ICT initiatives to an advocate of comprehensive digital development, to an active practitioner learning with a leading client, to more reflection and observation.

India remains a rich laboratory for digital innovation that can generate frugal development solutions and promote south-south knowledge and partnerships. It also remains a source for Bank learning and for sharing its experience with other countries via the Bank's learning platform.

CHAPTER 3

A First Integrated Transformation Project: e-Sri Lanka

Abstract This chapter describes in some depth a team's efforts to get the Bank to approve financial and technical assistance to a comprehensive e-Sri Lanka program, the Bank's first holistic digital transformation investment program. It was a pioneering program that faced many institutional hurdles at the Bank and client country. Bank's rigidities slowed down the mainstreaming of this innovation into digital development assistance. Many lessons were drawn during formulation and implementation of the program over 10 years.

Keywords Sri Lanka · Development strategy · Holistic digital strategy · Local ownership · Implementation

What were the origins of the first integrated Bank-funded digital transformation project? How did the joint vision of the government and Bank evolve over time? What were the main elements of this transformational project? How did country ownership and innovation capacity develop? How were implementation challenges addressed? What lessons can the Bank learn from transformational projects like this one? These questions kept me awake at night for two intense years until the Board approved the project in late 2004. Two book volumes (Hanna 2007a and 2008) describe the design and early implementation of the e-Sri Lanka project.

N. K. Hanna, *Driving Digital Transformation in Developing Nations*,
https://doi.org/10.1007/978-3-031-54573-3_3

Origins of e-Sri Lanka

The idea of e-Sri Lanka originated in the private sector, among the National Chamber of Commerce and local software industry leaders. The chamber prepared an early version of a national ICT road map, focusing mainly on developing the software industry. In parallel, local software associations worked with the US Agency for International Development (USAID) to support an ICT cluster.

Inspired by the success of the Indian software export industry over the previous decade, a 2002 report by USAID consultants proposed building a US$1 billion, export-focused software industry in five years (ICT Cluster Initiative 2002). This goal was to be achieved primarily through the development of digital parks and other government-supported initiatives. As per the report, this strategy would take advantage of local talent in software development, create jobs, and diversify exports. The ICT cluster would spur vigorous growth in an economy where traditional export industries of tea and textiles were facing stiff competition or losing global market share.

Sri Lanka's Minister of Science and Technology Milinda Moragoda took the proposal to the President of the World Bank, Wolfensohn, who in turn asked the Bank's chief information officer Muhsin to respond. These were unusual steps. They were prompted by the lack of a contact point within the Bank's mainstream lending operations. The client country was unsure about where to seek assistance for such an unusual cross-sectoral project within the Bank's complex bureaucracy. The global unit responsible for providing ICT operational assistance to client countries was then focusing on telecommunications infrastructure financing and regulation and skeptical about venturing beyond its traditional strengths and mandate. The CIO's office lacked the experience to offer operational assistance and lending and had no precedent or mandate to do so.

The First Mission to Sri Lanka

When testing the proposal informally with the Bank's internal stakeholders, the CIO heard much skepticism about Sri Lanka's aspiration to emulate India's software export drive, let alone to engage in digital transformation for broad economic success. Given Sri Lanka's development challenges, the proposal was deemed unrealistic and largely irrelevant.

About a decade earlier, in 1993, I conveyed a similar proposal from the Prime Minister of Sri Lanka that was rejected on similar grounds.

As the CIO (Mohamed Muhsin) was familiar with my advocacy and publications on national digital strategies, he asked me to take up the challenge, acknowledging that earlier attempts to fund comprehensive ICT strategies had been stymied within the Bank. Such assistance was viewed as a high-risk venture in an area where the Bank had no precedent or demonstrated competencies. The Bank's regional management agreed to a reconnaissance visit (mission) to Sri Lanka provided I would only have a small budget that remained unallocated for that FY and that further assistance was unlikely: "Do not come back with a project!". The regional management viewed the mission as a one-shot advisory service in response to a high-level request that could not be turned down. I was also advised that Sri Lanka had a poor project implementation record and would typically "ask for a Mercedes when they can only afford a bicycle"!

A team was quickly formed to visit the country. In recruiting team members, I looked for diverse perspectives and practical experience. An initial five-member team included an expert who came from Silicon Valley with software industry expertise and one from the Indian state of Andhra Pradesh for e-government expertise. External consultants were expected to carry credibility with the client, but knew little about the Bank's lending procedures and bureaucratic constraints. The rest of the team came from different parts of the Bank as there was no single focal point within the Bank with the needed mix of skills: a combination of prior knowledge of Sri Lanka's ICT sector and experience in developing and implementing holistic national digital strategies.

As the team leader, I could invite team members who were committed to the cause and client-centered, and who shared my vision of holistic e-development. The CIO agreed to second two young staff from the Development Gateway Foundation to add dynamism and cross-disciplinary perspectives to the team, for example, to devise a strategic communication program and a monitoring and evaluation system. I also reached out to the global ICT department for their in-depth expertise in telecommunications and affordable internet access solutions. It was not a ready-made team, as each had his/her expertise in only one element of the digital ecosystem. They were leaders in their own respective silos: telecommunications and internet access, shared access centers (telecenters), software industry development, and IT applications (e-government and e-society). There was little time for team building prior to our first mission to Sri

Lanka. Team solidarity was built up as we faced mounting resistance to our proposals upon return from the mission. Gaps in skills and differences in perspective—even within each silo—emerged along the way as we proceeded with follow-up missions and analyses.

My role was to focus attention on building new local leadership institutions, nurturing policy reforms, securing political ownership, responding to various stakeholders, developing synergies among program components, and defending the project against naysayers within the Bank. I also had to learn fast from the newly-constituted Bank team members, and particularly from our Sri Lankan counterparts.

Our country counterparts were not any better prepared to bridge their program components. They had to be recruited through an open and transparent competitive process, starting with the CEO of a proposed organization. The organization to host them did not yet exist, and no suitable home could be found in the existing institutional structure of government. The recruited staff were experts in their sectors (components) of a potential strategy, but none had ever designed and implemented an integrated national digital strategy. At that time (2002), a holistic digital strategy was a new concept, not commonly developed or executed. The CEO, with my support, had to build the Sri Lankan team from scratch and to encourage component program managers to work across their silos, specialties, and public–private links.

I spent my 18-hour flight from Washington to Sri Lanka without sleep, engrossed in a book on e-government. I was inspired by the holistic vision of a digital development ecosystem, and the challenge to make it happen. At that time, I was not a specialist in any single component of this ecosystem, except perhaps the policies to promote a local software services industry, the potential role of ICT in development, and national innovation systems. For me, it was more important to focus on the digital ecosystem as a whole, the interactions and complementarities among key components and their links to the overall development of the country. I was excited to help realize this vision.

In Sri Lanka, the mission came under intense pressure from key political and private sector leaders to promise visible and immediate actions and large funding for an ambitious but still undefined program. The private sector, having driven the original proposal, lobbied for a large share of the funding. Within the government, however, the sense of ownership seemed thin among senior civil servants. A few chief executive officers were engaged, including those of the Chamber of Commerce, the

Software Export Association, and a major telecommunications company. The early engagement of these stakeholders was consistent with the political leadership's vision of private sector-led services-based growth.

The mission's return with findings and recommendations opened a debate on digital development within the Bank and provided the first opportunity to form a position on a client's funding request for this purpose. The initial reaction reflected the prevailing skepticism at the Bank about the relevance of ICT to development. Some raised valid questions about whether it was appropriate for a government to support a private industry like ICT. Some claimed that the team was advocating a "discredited" industrial policy approach of intervening selectively and picking winners. Others felt that e-government should be pursued sector-by-sector or ministry-by-ministry, in line with the Bank's organization and sector-based lending.[1] Some saw a free-standing lending operation in the new field of ICT as competing with their sector-based budget allocations. Many questioned the feasibility of a comprehensive ICT strategy given skill limitations in both Sri Lanka and the Bank—they suggested a small pilot, if anything.

Launching the mission in response to a government request—before adding the project to the Bank's lending program and without extensive research and sector analysis was considered imprudent. The initiative may be driven by client priorities and international best practices, but how does it fit with standard sector-based reviews? How will management control a high-profile project beyond the Bank's traditional competencies? Some accused us of acting as cowboys! The chief economist for the Asia region asked why ICT development assistance was more important than supporting the textile or shoe industries. Were microchips more important than potato chips?!

Skeptics thought the ICT sector was just hype, especially in light of the early 2000s dot-com bubble burst. Stanford economist Kenneth Arrow's quip that "computers are everywhere, except in national productivity statistics" and the growing management literature about elusive productivity gains from ICT investments known as the "productivity paradox" added wood to the fire. The skeptics had their arguments ready. Are

[1] This is a key issue: Which aspects of ICT should be integrated into sectoral programs like education or rural development, and which treated as a coherent and independent program to build a whole-of-government ICT framework, with shared applications and infrastructure, and a common platform for enabling all sectors of the economy?

there any precedents from other countries? Even if they exist, can they be replicated? The skeptics insisted on major research prior to Bank commitment to such a visible project. And the research department would not touch such a controversial area (until 15 years later, for the 2016 World Development Report).

This management response was not unusual. As of 2002, ICT has not yet been mainstreamed into development practice. Other aid agencies working in established sectors—including the two major funding agencies in the region, the Asian Development Bank and the Japan Bank for International Cooperation—had similar reactions. At that time, USAID only wished to promote the ICT industry cluster and its private sector associations. Other bilateral donors failed to see the connection between ICT and achieving the UN's Millennium Development Goals of 2002. A few aid agencies, while sympathetic to Sri Lanka's aspirations, were skeptical about its ability to implement the program. A narrow definition of ICT's role in development and a rigid division of labor among donors in Sri Lanka did not help.

Gaining Traction, Changing Minds

I was determined to go ahead, basing my advocacy on mainly business literature. Forging an alliance with the Bank's country director for Sri Lanka proved critical. New management, arriving in Colombo in July 2002, soon after my first mission, sensed an unusually strong interest at the highest levels of government and business in seeking Bank assistance for this new and untested area. On its recommendation, the Bank's regional management allowed the project team to visit Sri Lanka with a slightly broader mandate—as long as it came back with a smaller and simpler program, perhaps just a pilot for the first phase, and as long as it addressed many of the constraints on ICT mainstreaming and practice in the Bank.

This challenge motivated me to build a strong team, this time with staff drawn from across the Bank—which proved critical in building ownership and alliances within the institution—as well as consultants with a broad range of expertise. The vision, the strong client interest, as well as the initial resistance within the Bank, all helped cement bonds among the new team members. It also helped to focus the team's efforts on mobilizing counterparts in Sri Lanka's political and business leadership and the emerging ICT field. I shared my passion for digital development with the team, and tried to protect the more junior and creative staff from the doubts and jealousies of the more traditional Bank specialists.

The choice of a local manager with passion for technological transformation and private sector experience to lead the proposed national ICT Agency (ICTA), proved to be a key success factor. The first CEO of ICTA helped recruit and shape the local Sri Lankan team into a highly motivated group, with diverse backgrounds and strong project management experience. The local team also grew with the challenges it faced energized by the political interest in a new theme for unifying the country.

E-Sri Lanka offered a unique opportunity to take Bank assistance in this area to the next level and to learn from best practices in leveraging ICT to accelerate national development, boost competitiveness, and alleviate information poverty.[2] Opportunities came with tough choices. The e-Sri Lanka program was tentatively estimated at US$500 million, with US$300 million to come from the private sector and, it was hoped, US$100 million from the Bank. Despite the apparent funding constraints, the client ruled out the option of starting with a pilot and then gradually moving to a full-blown program. That led to some tough decisions on priorities: What should the minimal core elements of the program be? Where can other aid agencies get involved via co-financing and export credit? What should be piloted first, or phased in over time? How can the claims of different stakeholders be balanced?

Awareness of financial constraints proved to be a blessing. It saved the Bank's project team from falling into the trap of developing a vision and strategy document without realistic funding and implementation prospects. It also helped the counterpart team in setting priorities and making choices, and thus avoid overstretching the nascent capacity of ICTA that was expected to manage a complex and interdependent investment program.

A key decision at that point was to focus on connectivity and e-government programs, which would require lumpy investments for critical infrastructure, platforms, and systems. For connectivity, having a regional focus within Sri Lanka was deemed necessary. This would have the dual advantage of accommodating funding constraints and deepening the focus on the poorer regions of the country. Similarly, for e-government,

[2] On how ICT can increase competitiveness and alleviate information poverty, see Mody and Dahlman (1992) and Hanna (1991).

focusing on shared platforms (like the country portal and government-wide intranet) would meet funding constraints and avoid premature involvement in large ICT applications in specific sectors. Another critical decision was to focus on human resources and training essential to the implementation of the first phase of the program, while leaving the vast area of ICT in education (and education in ICT) to a follow-up project with the Ministry of Education.[3]

As word about the project and client feedback spread throughout the Bank and the program design gained credibility, it became easier for the new regional Bank leadership to support an initiative that had already gained some traction. Some colleagues were quick to see the potential complementarities between e-Sri Lanka and their sectors, for example, for using community information centers (telecenters) to deliver agricultural extension and information-based rural development services. This turnaround was neither instant nor dramatic. It took time to persuade people to adopt new ideas and for these ideas to filter down through the organization. In large aid bureaucracies, incentives for innovation are weak and errors of commission account for more than errors of omission.

Building Local Capacity and Ownership

The next phase was to build local capacity and initiate project formulation while navigating political pressures and changing expectations. The Bank team lacked full-time counterparts in Sri Lanka. We often met our counterparts late in the evening after they were done with their day jobs. This was a challenge especially with managing director of the National Development Bank Eran Wickramaratne and senior advisor to the Minister of Science and Technology Milinda Moragoda. Both Eran and Milinda created the early vision of the role of ICT in the economic and national development of the country. Eran was my main counterpart in the project. He was so busy I had to bring him extensive reports to our late-night meetings at the end of my missions in the hope that he skims through them. There was no established ministry or agency to follow up on mission findings and recommendations. Thus, the first priority was

[3] The Ministry of Education and public universities were judged to be slow to change, the minister was from a rival party, and major aid agencies worked with the ministry rather independently. Because of this, keeping its programs out of e-Sri Lanka was judged to conserve on coordination efforts as well.

to set up a governance mechanism through the establishment of an ICT agency.

The low level of ICT awareness and among parliament members made gaining parliamentary approval for the creation of a new agency a challenge. In 2003, the Parliament finally passed the ICT law, so the next step was to recruit the agency CEO and key program managers. Positions were advertised to ensure competitive bidding and attracting Sri Lankans, including those working overseas. Creating and staffing the ICT Agency was key to localizing project management and building a true partnership between local stakeholders and the Bank.

The newly created ICT Agency faced daunting challenges. Its staff had no experience with preparing a program of this size or with meeting Bank requirements for project preparation and procurement. Manju, the CEO, came from the private sector, bringing a business culture to this public agency, but he lacked experience working with government and aid agencies. He had to acquire this knowledge fast, even while recruiting his team, piloting quick-impact projects, and preparing the e-Sri Lanka program for Bank financing.

The Bank team developed a project management tool laying out the many steps needed to prepare the program in line with the Bank's rigorous requirements for financing. It hoped to overcome skepticism among local partners and aid agencies. Luckily, many of the new staff were familiar with project management tools and quickly internalized the steps, adapting and improving them.

The next big turning point occurred at the time of national elections in April 2004 that the opposition unexpectedly won. In the run-up to the elections the e-Sri Lanka program and the ICT Agency were under constant attack.[4] But discreet efforts to reach out to the opposition and address both misunderstandings and legitimate concerns before the elections paid off when the opposition won. Moreover, strategically selected early pilots targeting the ICT needs of the Parliament, the President, and

[4] Rumor had it that the telecenters were to serve only members of certain religious groups. Critics cited the lack of immediate results on the ground, even though Bank funding for the program had not yet been approved. Others focused on perceptions that e-Sri Lanka catered to the interests of the private sector rather than poverty reduction. Questions were raised about the composition of the agency staff (education, class, ethnicity, and religious affiliations) and about whether staffing and salaries suggested an elitist organization, inconsistent with the ideology of the main opposition party at the time.

the Cabinet helped raise awareness and promote ownership of e-Sri Lanka among key political officials.

Our experience confirmed the importance of pilot projects, coalition building, and strategic communications in creating the "authorizing environment"—the mandate of an organization and its political and legal support (for detailed discussion of this concept, see Moore 1998). It also suggested that the authorizing environment demands continuous attention and maintenance, particularly in a turbulent political environment like Sri Lanka's.

Prior sector and situational analysis and deeper knowledge of country institutions also mattered, provided such analysis was timely, locally owned, and actionable. But perhaps more important was getting close to the client and ultimate project beneficiaries and finding ways to capture knowledge as it emerged from interactions with different actors, from political dynamics, from early pilots, and from multiple feedback mechanisms.

Once the new government was in place, a bureaucratic fight over where the ICT Agency should be located within the administration broke out. The Bank could only keep its ears to the ground and emphasize the need to secure autonomy and authority for the ICT Agency, maintain the integrity of the program, and allow for the flexibility to address the new government's priorities of rural development and poverty reduction.

By then it was mainly a local game. Luckily, the ICT Agency was agile enough to influence the outcome. The newly elected government clearly attached significance to the e-Sri Lanka program, holding the first negotiations with the Bank in the Prime Minister's office. It positioned the ICT Agency to report to the prime minister's office, reflecting a growing understanding of the program's cross-cutting nature.

Thus, the design of the e-Sri Lanka program survived a major political shift almost intact.

Growing Ownership at the Bank

Internally, managing the new lending operation outside of the South Asia regional unit, and outside of the Global ICT department presented its own difficulties. Free-standing lending operations are seldom managed outside of the Bank's regional units where traditional sector expertise lies. Telecommunications has been the exception, viewed as a highly specialized technical area that needs little coordination or integration with other sectors within the Bank's regional structure. With no regional or central home in the Bank, this new type of assistance had to be managed from the CIO's office, even though this office was neither adequately positioned to lead lending operations nor to get specialized expertise from support functions such as procurement and disbursement.

This presented a dilemma for Bank management. The innovation represented by the e-Sri Lanka program was unlikely to sprout from within the regional structure, given the prevailing skill mix and the substantial upfront R&D investment required for a transformational project. But in the long run, it could not survive and grow without a home in that structure.

As negotiations between the Bank and the Sri Lankan government went ahead with the project pending Bank Board approval, internal changes were afoot to absorb the ICT "sector" into the South Asia regional structure. The regional VP for South Asia, Praful Patel, declared regional support for ICT as a key infrastructure for Asia's economies. This top management support was critical in a hierarchical, risk-averse organization. This commitment was confirmed after other South Asian client countries requested Bank assistance for projects similar to e-Sri Lanka. As the e-Sri Lanka program began to provide a common framework for ICT investment and technical assistance, several other aid agencies expressed interest in collaboration and financing. All this helped reinforce South Asia regional unit's ownership of the e-Sri Lanka program.

Prior to Board approval, I was back and forth to Sri Lanka working to secure government commitment. One night I got a surprise email from my boss, the CIO, informing me of his intention to relocate me from his front office to the systems department. The visibility of e-Sri Lanka caused rivalry between the CIO's systems department and the South Asia regional management that wanted to lead this promising project. I believed that the project demanded a high degree of authority and autonomy to allow for innovation and cut across turfs within the Bank. I agreed with Bank management that I would leave my job after the presentation to the Board. I promised to consult when needed and to write a book on e-Sri Lanka to guide future TTLs.

When I presented the e-Sri Lanka project to the Bank's Board of Executive Directors in September 2004, President Wolfensohn who chaired the discussion said he has been waiting for a project like this for the last ten years, he urged mainstreaming the comprehensive approach to digital transformation taken by the Bank and country leadership. The

Board endorsed the program despite concerns about its ambitious scope and the untested ICTA. In fact, Board members wanted similar projects in countries they represented, rich and poor alike. The regional management team committed to build their capacity to mainstream this innovation in response to client requests.

The Evolution of the e-Sri Lanka Program[5]

In spite of Sri Lanka's aspirations, proximity to major digital technology centers in India and East Asia, and a promising pool of ICT professionals, several factors constrained its digital development. These included: (i) poor coordination of ICT-related policies and programs; (ii) a low level of ICT use within government and among SMEs; (iii) an SME-dominated ICT services industry lacking institutional support for finance and marketing; (iv) low digital literacy; (v) communication infrastructure concentrated in urban areas; (vi) lack of public access points (telecenters) to make the Internet affordable to the majority of the population; and (vii) an underdeveloped legal and cybersecurity environment to create trust in electronic transactions. The e-Lanka project sought to address these challenges in a coherent way in support of the overall development of the country.

The Bank team worked with Sri Lankan counterparts to articulate several key project development outcomes (PDOs) to address the challenges and aspirations:

- Effective, citizen-centered, and business-friendly government;
- Empowerment of the rural poor, disabled, women, and youth through increased and affordable access to information and communication tools;
- Developed leadership and skills in ICT; and
- Employment creation through the ICT industry and digitally-enabled services, and enhanced competitiveness of user industries and services.

[5] The experience was documented in two published books (Hanna 2007, 2008).

There was no blueprint strategy or model program to address these PDOs. The emerging outline of e-Sri Lanka program covered six basic components:

- *ICT policy, leadership, and institutional development*—a policy development and capacity-building program to create an enabling environment for the knowledge economy and develop local institutional capacity to lead and implement an ambitious ICT program. Leadership was principally located within the ICTA, empowered by an independent board of directors drawn from the public and private sectors.
- *Human resource development and digital industry* innovation fund—to build ICT human resource capacity and create jobs in the dynamic ICT sector, foreign and local investment in the sector, and diffusion of ICT among SMEs. The ICT Capacity-Building Fund was to use competitive grants and contracting on a fee-for-service basis to fund subprograms and studies.
- *Regional telecommunications network development*—a least-cost subsidy scheme to extend the digital infrastructure and connectivity to serve the poorest regions of the country. The program was expected to promote competitive and affordable telecommunications services for users, particularly the poorer segments of society, and was expected to integrate communities throughout the country, providing appropriate channels for e-government, e-commerce, and e-learning services. The network was to connect 200 telecenters (shared access and services centers).
- *Rural connectivity and telecenter development*—targeted subsidy and entrepreneurial development schemes to develop affordable access to the Internet, ICT tools, digital literacy, local content, digital government services, and e-commerce applications—utilizing the new digital infrastructure, e-government applications, and a grassroots-oriented innovation fund to serve SMEs, farmers, students, women, youth, and other marginalized groups. Voucher schemes were expected to augment demand from target populations. The program was also expected to contain a community outreach component that was expected to enable distance learning for the target population, computer literacy training for teachers in rural areas, and use of the telecenters by rural secondary schools. Grassroots initiatives

were expected to generate telecenter services to be funded under an e-Society Fund program.

- *Societal innovation (e-society)*—an innovation fund to mobilize local knowledge, digitize and share local content, and use ICT for social development, grassroots participation, and empowerment of the poor. Competitive grants were expected to fund pilot projects implemented by community organizations, NGOs, private companies, and public and social-sector institutions.
- *Digital (Reengineering) government*—a coherent investment program in digital platforms and applications, information sharing, knowledge management, process reengineering, service innovation, and human resources to deliver faster, more efficient, and more transparent government services to all citizens and businesses.

The design of the e-Sri Lanka program aimed to capture key synergies among these programs. A newly created national e-leadership institution, the ICT Agency, was designed, authorized, and equipped to realize these synergies and to partner with other stakeholders to create an ecosystem for leveraging ICT for development. Monitoring and evaluation systems were designed to promote coordination across the entire program, maximizing learning and adaptation throughout its implementation.

Project preparation started in July 2002 with the development of pilots and the creation and staffing of the ICT Agency using the project preparation financing facility (PPF). Project financing of about US$ 55 million was approved in late 2004. The design and management of the program were flexible enough to permit adaptation and reprogramming in view of emerging gaps and the need to consolidate high-impact pilots and initiatives. Additional financing of US$11 million was approved near project completion to scale up project impact. The Bank-assisted project was completed in 2013.

Guiding Principles for Engagement

As a team, we strived to adhere to some key principles to guide the preparation of the e-Sri Lanka program. These principles drew on lessons of development assistance that I learned while working with various client countries and from management literature, as well as the growing literature on "new development economics."

- *Taking a holistic, long-term, and development-driven view*—to ensure that the national digital strategy is driven by the larger national development strategy and by development outcomes, not ICT investments, and to tap complementarities with other development programs as well as synergies within the e-Sri Lanka program.
- *Securing broad local ownership among key stakeholders*—to create and implement a sustainable, cross-cutting program.
- *Adopting a knowledge-based partnership*—to ensure ownership, knowledge transfer, capacity building, local innovation, sustainable institutional change, and a good fit with local conditions.
- *Ensuring programmatic flexibility*—to accommodate scarce upfront information, an uncertain political environment, untested capabilities, and adapt to unanticipated implementation challenges and fast-changing technologies.
- *Promoting bottom-up initiatives*—to accommodate complexity and diversity, to stimulate innovation, to build partnerships for social learning, and to complement top-down strategic directions.
- *Funding quick-results pilots*—to nurture political commitment and social learning.
- *Building multiple feedback mechanisms*—to support just-in-time learning and local innovation as well as institutionalize monitoring and evaluation.

Beneath all the success factors was perhaps the most fundamental one: understanding the local situation, the stakeholders, the political economy, and the broader context of development. For example, securing local ownership and developing a coalition of stakeholders required knowing who the stakeholders were, what incentives they responded to, and what perspectives they held. There was no clear or static "list" of stakeholders. It often changed as the program developed—and in response to its development. Similarly, developing a knowledge-based partnership required an awareness of local knowledge sources, such as local think tanks to partner with. Launching pilots to deliver quick results implied an understanding of local needs to assess which pilots were likely to have the most impact on key stakeholders.

To illustrate, I take one of these principles as applied to e-Sri Lanka: promoting bottom-up Initiatives. As initial program preparation unfolded, different stakeholders demanded resources to meet *their* urgent need for ICT investments or to promote *their* segment of the ICT industry. Proposals were springing up from the private sector, civil society, and academic and training institutions. Our strategy encouraged such bottom-up initiatives, but the government lacked a mechanism for aggregating and prioritizing these demands and for engaging as a partner in the many local initiatives, let alone for learning from them and mainstreaming promising local innovations. The ICT Agency had to focus on large, strategic investments, and overall program management, it could not dissipate its limited capacity on appraising many small grassroots initiatives.

A search for appropriate mechanisms to simultaneously aggregate and prioritize these demands, simplify program management, and maximize learning led to the idea of creating two national funds. One, the *ICT industry promotion and capacity building fund* would promote innovations to meet the ICT industry's human resource development needs, to develop the domestic market, and to promote the country as a digitally-enabled service exporter. The other, the *e-society fund*, would promote grassroots innovation and community capacity to use ICT for poverty reduction and social development.

These types of mechanisms to support bottom-up initiatives also aim to promote innovative partnerships across the public–private divide. Thus, the two funds were also established to enable the public, business, academic, and civil society sectors to partner on ICT skills upgrade and to leverage ICT for poverty reduction and community development. Such cross-sectoral partnerships were critical to promote policy reforms, social learning, and sustainable institutional change.

Implementation Experience

The program evolved throughout the implementation process and in response to the fluid political environment. It survived multiple changes in Bank staffing, the departure of ICTA's CEO, and the politically motivated replacement of ICTA's board. An independent evaluation at project completion rated the program and government performance as *satisfactory* and, in some areas—even exceeding original ambitious targets.[6]

[6] A World Bank evaluation, the Project Implementation and Results Report (2014), provides details of implementation performance and results.

Early attention to building ICTA capacity proved critical to the survival of the program as it had to adapt to political priorities and rely on local innovation. ICTA's monitoring and evaluation system kept evolving. The "deliberate strategy" design proved to be a robust game plan that unfolded along with an "emergent" strategy borne out of constant testing on the ground.

Bank performance, however, was independently rated *moderately unsatisfactory*, and this may have made the country director reluctant to commit to continued Bank support through follow-up projects. Regional management wanted to take over, but the regional unit lacked the skills and resources to manage a new learning-intensive project. The unit focused on private sector development but lacked ICT sector knowledge. It was not well-positioned to cover a cross-sectoral, innovative project.

The frequent TTL turnover sent mixed signals and led to conflicting interpretations of Bank policies and procedures. As new ambitious TTLs arrived, there were no mechanisms in place to protect innovation, secure continuity, and support cumulative institutional learning. ICTA staff complained about having to spend too much time "educating" new TTLs on setting realistic targets and working around rigid Bank requirements. The last TTL was a financial sector expert prone to micromanaging procurement. Instead of building trust and learning together with the ICTA team, he bullied and dictated. ICTA was working in a nascent and highly dynamic sector covering over a hundred small contracts and pilots with small enterprises in poor communities where rigid Bank practices would be counterproductive—they needed agile and learning-oriented Bank "supervision."

ICTA staff had to learn on their own. Despite VP Praful's desire to take on this new cross-sectoral challenge, the regional unit failed to build the required competencies, and did not get much support from the global ICT department. The Sri Lankan Office of the President would often ask my management to engage me to resolve critical issues with the Bank. I enjoyed the challenge and the trust I established with both sides. But I could not substitute for the Bank building its own capabilities to partner and learn with the client. This was an opportunity for the Bank to learn from a transformational project for the benefit of other countries. An opportunity it missed.

The E-society program was perhaps the most visible digital inclusion component of the program. It promoted innovative use of ICT to address the needs of rural areas and the most vulnerable populations through community and partnership grants. Among its pilots were reaching out to the disabled, improving fishermen's incomes, developing relevant local content for telecenters, including online materials for rural students, and "smart village" applications.

The e-Society program supported pilots through a small grant from the e-Sri Lanka program. We hoped successful pilots would bring new partners to co-fund the program, invest in promising pilots, and scale them at the national level. The e-society fund was envisaged as a social venture capital fund for applying ICT to social and rural development, and for building awareness more widely about the relevance of ICT for poverty reduction and growth.

Scaling and mainstreaming grassroots innovation was a challenge. This required collaboration with the government, the private sector and NGO to widen distribution channels for e-society solutions. Grassroots organizations had to build capacity to host content, while the donor community and ICT multinationals had to help replicate successful pilots. In other words, this was a major institutional innovation that could have led to community-driven broad-based digital transformation. To realize its full potential, however, more resources and attention should have been invested into social marketing and dissemination by development partners in the public and private sectors.

Achievement of Development Objectives

e-Sri Lanka's development project objectives (PDOs) focused on economy-wide indicators (inequality, growth, and employment) that went beyond what a project of this nature could achieve and created an inherent problem of results attribution. These PDOs were set in response to government expectations, in spite of the skepticism that the design team faced within the Bank and the lack of quantitative assessment of the digital economy and baseline data on more specific indicators. The PDOs were nevertheless well aligned with the scope of the project and thus a reasonable way to gauge its performance that the Bank's Independent Evaluation Group (IEG) rated as satisfactory.

Aside from the high-level indicators, the project has certainly contributed to significant improvements in delivery of government services, including common processes such as online tax filing, railway bookings, and driver license renewal. These are significant in and of themselves, yet they also impacted the creation of critical e-government infrastructure, equity, capacity building, efficiency, transparency, and growth. Over the years, engaging with the Bank led to technical knowledge transfer and implementation support, and a certain degree of ICTA autonomy.

There is reason to believe that the project helped create a platform that enabled the growth of the ICT industry and public services in Sri Lanka that was reflected in global rankings of the UN, the WEF, the Bill and Melinda Gates Foundation, etc.[7] Sri Lanka's ICT literacy rate rose from 4% at the start of the project in 2004 to 35% at its end in 2014.

The project supported the development of the digital sector. ICTA was instrumental in helping the government strengthen its policy framework for the digital economy. It led to the successful unification of the eight ICT industry associations and helped create a promising coalition of software and BPO companies. ICTA also helped public agencies to manage their own digital transformation. The position of a national Chief Innovation Officer (CIO) was established with a staff mandated to promote ICT usage within their respective government agencies.

The project contributed to social development, with a special emphasis on using ICT to integrate the poorest populations of the South and North East regions of the country. To encourage broad participation, government stakeholders were engaged in the e-Policy, Leadership and Institutional Development Program, and the Reengineering Government Program while business and academia focused on the ICT Human Resources Development and Industry Promotion. Synergies between telecommunications, telecenters, e-government, and e-society programs were encouraged to render information access and service provision to rural populations.

[7] For instance, Sri Lanka was awarded the Outsourcing Destination of the Year by the National Outsourcing Association (NOA), UK in 2013 and 2014. It was ranked in the top 10 most improved countries for doing business in 2013, in the top 25 global outsourcing destinations by AT Kearney, and in the top 30 outsourcing destinations by Gartner. It ranked the 5th in ICT (2005/06) development between (2005/06 and 2011/12) globally, as reported by the World Economic Forum in its Global Information Technology Report 2011/2012, and it is continuing to improve (2014/2015). In the UN e-Gov Index rankings, Sri Lanka went from 116 to 75 out of 192 countries in 2014. e-Sri Lanka's telecentre (Nenasala) program was chosen for the Bill & Melinda Gates' Access to Learning Award in 2014 out of 200 applicants from 115 countries.

The project affected all participating organizations including ICTA, ministries, and other government agencies. A new institution was built from scratch, attracting new talent and introducing business practices to government. It also brought about systemic change in the culture and effective use of ICT by several ministries, government agencies, and private sector institutions.

We hoped that the e-Sri Lanka project umbrella would accelerate the roll-out of ongoing and planned project components in a variety of sectors such as education, poverty reduction, and reconstruction. Activities sponsored through other Bank projects were expected to be substantially strengthened by (a) improving access to information and communication tools which promoted content provision at central government and local levels; (b) strengthening the ICT industry and education; and (c) developing a common information and communication platform for the whole economy.

Despite these achievements, the future of Sri Lanka's digital transformation remains uncertain. Political leadership is essential to continuity and sustained results. ICTA's institutional design was meant to create a relatively autonomous yet accountable and professional technocracy, but the agency alone cannot lead the digital transformation of the entire economy, and particularly of the government, without supportive and inclusive political and technocratic leadership.

Lessons from e-Sri Lanka

The e-Sri Lanka project was learning intensive, as any transformational project in a new economic sector would be. It was an encouraging start in a long digital transformation journey with uncertainties, ups, and downs. Long-lasting impact of digital transformation will depend on political leadership, commitment to reform, capacity building and learning by Sri Lanka and its development partners.

I learned a lot from this rich and long engagement with a country: the importance of: inspiring local stakeholders with a vision, establishing partnerships, promoting local learning and innovation, supporting and nurturing stakeholder ownership, and mainstreaming digital transformation in development assistance. In the following, I sum up these lessons.

The first lesson I learned is the importance of developing an inspiring vision of digital transformation and clarifying its relevance to economic development. Creating such a vision involves leadership development, coalition formation, capacity building, and institutional development to move from e-vision to e-strategy to e-program implementation. I resisted using a blueprint approach and artificial precision in design and implementation. An exciting vision helped bring talent to ICTA. The initial Board of ICTA—composed of diverse stakeholders from the public, private, and academic/NGO sectors—endowed the CEO with enough space to propose, mobilize, and innovate. The CEO and ICTA teams were encouraged to improve and reshape the initial vision in the process of planning and implementation. I observed the teams and focus groups at work, and learned with them to take advantage of their full potential. In many ways, the Bank role was to bring uncodified global knowledge for an emerging sector driven by fast-changing technology.

Digitally-enabled development required balancing short- and long-term outcomes. Sustained commitment to a new vision of development needs visible interim progress, but digital transformation is not a quick technological fix. E-Sri Lanka presented neither a perfect design nor a final solution to the challenges of integrating digital technologies in development. To me it was the start of a journey of profound change. True transformation always involves creative destruction, risks, and uncertainties. The long-term outcome depends on political factors well beyond a single project. Managing expectations about short-term outcomes proved difficult as incentives were not always aligned to manage for the long term.

Initially, the Bank and country teams envisioned this program as a long-term partnership in sync with Sri Lanka's digital transformation journey. The Bank team emphasized the need for partnership not only with ICTA, but also with concerned ministries, the private sector, and civil society. Many internal management factors within the Bank and political-institutional factors in Sri Lanka made these partnerships difficult to create. Initially, the Bank team and the government convinced the country director of the need for assistance in this new area. Subsequently, the director played a crucial role in providing a focal point for Bank dialogue and overcoming the resistance of competing managers from more established sectors. Early on, the team argued that e-Sri Lanka should be viewed not as a new sector that competes for aid, but as a provider of platforms and enabling policies for digitization and transformation of all key sectors of the country. Frequent changes in country directors in favor of risk-averse and skeptical individuals undermined the effectiveness of the Bank in this nascent area. Similar changes in the Bank team and its country counterparts along with a short-term approach of coalition governments prevented the establishment of long-term relations in this rapidly emerging sector.

Empowerment had to extend beyond the core agency—to involve its partners. Public–private partnerships and incentives were needed to bridge the digital divide and accelerate rural connectivity. Empowerment also required a process to reach national consensus on component strategies and to prioritize investment in e-government services and process change initiatives. Extending beyond its turf was not a natural or easy way for ICTA to adopt. As a new organization in an uncertain authorizing environment, it needed to build its reputation by delivering results in the short term and taking credit for new services. Moreover, its potential partners were also newcomers to partnering and managing their own digital transformation. Capacity building for partners and stakeholders was necessary to keep ICTA small, agile, and focused.

An integrated approach to digital development also requires coordination and integration capabilities among stakeholder institutions. It calls for an upfront effort to build local capacity, partnerships, and outsourcing practices, and internalize a holistic approach to digital transformation. We expected that Bank implementation assistance would support synergies and complementarities rather than fragmented pilots and isolated digital development components.

The second lesson is the need to innovate, adapt, and learn to realize the potential benefits of digital technologies. Initially, we used some of the preparation funds for piloting small, quick-win ICT applications to demonstrate value to key stakeholders. Once project funding was approved, it incorporated several innovation funds to promote the software industry, diffuse ICT among small enterprises, invest in human resources for the information society, and promote societal applications that would target marginalized groups. The project teams thus developed mechanisms to balance top-down strategies with bottom-up initiatives to support local innovation. The aim was to build community capacity to use ICT to solve local development problems, and to diffuse promising innovations. Scaling innovations, however, proved too demanding, and at times ICTA was unable to persuade public agencies to diffuse promising innovations.

E-Sri Lanka was both a learning process and a destination. It was about learning to learn. A transformative program that is built on experimentation typically requires intensive learning by both the aid agency and local stakeholders. While there was growing awareness of the importance of experimentation and innovation in development programs, there was less willingness to provide the necessary resources to learn and adapt. The tacit knowledge generated should be systematically captured and shared. Local monitoring and evaluation is key to capture and share lessons, and scale and sustain transformational change.

Together with the CIO and Bank colleagues, we tried to disseminate lessons gained from the project during the design and implementation phases. I helped create a community of practice for e-development that provided a forum to share emerging lessons from the project. We leveraged the then new tools of videoconferencing to reach out to other interested countries to exchange experiences.

Excitement aside, innovation was not easy, especially for Sri Lanka's overstaffed and politicized civil service and for large aid agencies like the Bank. Despite expressed top management interest, risk aversion was the norm at the Bank. Bank staff are usually committed and competitive. But they also know the price of failure that often accompanies innovation. The risks are multiplied for pioneering new sectors where external and internal coalitions for change are too weak to protect the pioneers. Social innovators and entrepreneurs are not encouraged to apply!

The third lesson is the need to nurture local ownership of innovative and adaptive digital transformation programs. Local ownership matters especially when dealing with digital transformation as digital dividends depend on profound socio-technical change and complementary adaptation of institutions and skills. Digital transformation cuts across all economic sectors and has no natural home in the government system. In Sri Lanka, Milinda, Eran, and Lalit played different but critical roles in promoting political ownership. Post-election government changes shifted program priorities from growth and private sector focus to rural development and e-society, and back again. Turnover in government leadership led to changes in ICTA governance and shifts in program components. Thus, local ownership was fluid and had to be sustained to survive all these changes.

Ownership had to be built top down to deal with interdependencies at the ecosystem level, and bottom-up to promote grassroots innovations and tap local knowledge to adapt ICT applications to the local context.

Understanding local stakeholders, from avid change leaders to those in need of a helping hand to those who had to be won over or neutralized was a challenge. We hoped that pilots would demonstrate the value of digital transformation to all involved and strengthen local ownership.

The biggest challenge was to gain and sustain public sector ownership. Sri Lanka had perhaps the highest level of per capita civil servants and the highest number of ministries. The top level of the civil service was highly politicized. Lalit, the most senior civil servant, was passionate about improving public service delivery and digital government. Similarly, Wasantha Deshapriya, e-government program director at ICTA, tried to facilitate the adoption of e-government solutions, while keeping the line ministries in charge of their own transformation processes. Ownership had to be nurtured agency by agency. Shared digital infrastructures, platforms, and data standards had to be owned collectively across the entire government. ICTA had to play a proactive role to secure adoption of best practices in process reengineering, and to move forward in collaboration with the Ministry of Public Administration.

E-Sri Lanka program ownership within the Bank was no less challenging. The original team I led had to change after my departure from the Bank. The South Asia region and the central ICT department clashed over leadership. Frequent TTL rotations weakened Bank ownership and lowered the trust between Bank and client teams. Internal Bank tensions distracted teams from partnering with the client. The resident country director also changed and his replacements were unable to sustain the strong country ownership they inherited.

The final lesson is the need to mainstream digital transformation in development practice. The design process of complex and innovative projects like e-Sri Lanka generates substantial practical knowledge, but this knowledge is seldom codified and shared. The "not invented here syndrome" should be overcome. While digital development strategies must be tailored to country specificities, the design of the e-Sri Lanka program and institutions is generic and can be applied broadly. Operational research and development (R&D) conducted by the Bank and the government of Sri Lanka can be valuable to other practitioners. This R&D can inform much-needed awareness raising and training for aid agencies, country policymakers, and academic institutions. It can also be helpful to those providing technical assistance or marketing information technology services.

The e-Sri Lanka experience highlights many development assistance challenges. As a new and disruptive dimension of development, digital transformation demands new local development policies, institutions, and capabilities to help transform established sectors and entrenched business practices. It also requires knowledge-based partnerships between aid agencies and local stakeholders. It calls for programmatic flexibility and agile implementation which in turn calls for trust and knowledge sharing between the country and its development partners. It requires long-term perspectives and strategic partnerships. Aid agencies have to develop the necessary frameworks and practices to act as learners, collaborators, co-innovators, risk-takers, strategic partners, and informed and honest brokers.

The e-Sri Lanka project catalyzed transformational change. It demanded a quantum leap in performance. It also called for sustained commitment to a comprehensive vision—a vision that underscored the potential promises, which were plentiful, but also acknowledged the critical choices that had to be made, the potential risks to be managed, and the coalitions to be nurtured and sustained along the way.

It set "stretch goals" to mobilize support within the government, the private sector, civil society, and the Bank. It supported deep and sustainable change with the potential for broad impact. It employed different modes of engagement, including lending and knowledge partnerships. It benefitted from the early engagement of local champions and visionaries as well as effective program managers, knowledgeable local consultants, and committed partners. Implementation success was based on local institutions and capabilities. It addressed many of the constraints and foundations of the digital transformation ecosystem and catalyzed local innovation. It aimed to share global knowledge and adapt programmatic interventions to local context.

The e-Sri Lanka project helped place digital transformation at the heart of the country's development agenda. Sri Lanka had to become a fast learner and join the technological race.

It is hard to over-emphasize the importance of governance and political leadership to digital transformation success. Despite all the mutually-agreed steps to secure ICTA's professional independence, its performance in core program areas like digital government depended on stable political leadership. Dramatic changes in the political environment undercut its project performance. E-Sri Lanka was not expected to substitute for responsible country governance, yet it hoped to minimize the politicization of digital government institutions. During project implementation in 2005–2012, Bank assistance offered some safeguards, but the Bank did not adequately engage after project completion in 2012. Nevertheless, ICTA and e-Sri Lanka made significant progress in what was expected to be a long and challenging journey.

CHAPTER 4

Transforming Government

Abstract This chapter explores the broad theme: *open government* (demand for good government, DFGG). In an era of growing political and economic polarization, can the DFGG movement strengthen the demand for transparent, responsive, and effective government? Will digital technologies help develop responsive government or reinforce existing public service divides? Governance and country contexts are critical to the outcomes of deploying digital technologies in the public sector. This chapter distills the challenges of deploying digital technologies for open and accountable government. It emphasizes political commitment and public leadership competencies. Kenya's Open Data Initiative is examined for lessons and best practices for other developing countries.

Keyword Open government · Open data · Responsive public services · Governance · Country context · Kenya

In 2012, the Bank's regional management in Africa requested my advice on promoting the emerging WBG practice of using ICT to improve public services and governance in Africa. It was just as the "Arab Spring" raised expectations about government transparency, accountability, and responsiveness to citizen demand for good government (DFGG). My colleagues and I were swept by the euphoria surrounding open data, open

N. K. Hanna, *Driving Digital Transformation in Developing Nations*, https://doi.org/10.1007/978-3-031-54573-3_4

government, and the new social contract between the government and its citizens. Could the latest digital technologies shift the dynamics of digital government from top-down supply of complex systems to grassroots-driven innovation and government accountability? Would this lead to more collaboration among ICT, governance, and social development practices within aid agencies?

As a result of this engagement, I authored a paper that aimed to explore and raise awareness of the current state and potential of using ICT as a means to increase transparency and accountability, as well as to enhance civic participation in governance across Africa (Hanna 2012). The engagement was driven by the rapid spread of mobile and smartphones and related applications. It was also motivated by the urgent need to improve service delivery to support the fragile political, economic, and social environments in Africa.

I started with documenting rapid grassroots innovations that leveraged ICT for good governance and provided a strategic framework for the broad categories of government functions where ICT could be applied. I was impressed by the African grassroots innovation explosion. The challenge was to scale and sustain it. This engagement also taught me about social intermediaries and their role in promoting open and transparent government, and responsive and inclusive public services.

My paper went beyond a narrow focus on technology to demonstrate the critical importance of understanding the sociopolitical context and the enabling policies and institutions that would best leverage new technologies. National ICT ecosystems can provide effective entry points for governments and development partners to work on leveraging digital technologies for good governance and effective service delivery. The paper identified the key challenges—particularly sociopolitical and institutional—to the broad adoption of ICT for governance and service delivery. It proposed a set of recommendations to overcome these.

Governance and public sector capacity were considered the foundation of the Bank's then new Africa strategy. The governance challenge in Africa was particularly acute. State performance was disappointingly weak, putting further progress on development goals at risk. Results of interventions on the supply side alone have often been disappointing, so strengthening DFGG was a logical step. Africa's sociopolitical evolution and economic development required a more balanced approach between supply and demand. Inspired by the Arab Spring, President Zoellick's 2011 speech suggested that the Bank was ready to "modernize" its approach to development and place governance, citizen empowerment, and institutional reform at its heart.

As I prepared to engage with Africa, I researched ways ICT could be deployed to *improve public sector efficiency and accountability for resource management*. These included:

- Modernizing public finance and expenditure management systems, making them transparent, and tracking budgets online and through mobile phones.
- Mapping and monitoring the needs and resources of poor communities with mobile and geo-mapping technologies.
- Opening public procurement systems for fair competition and accountability by using electronic procurement applications and engaging social intermediaries.
- Modernizing tax systems and revenue administration to raise revenues while reducing corruption and tax avoidance.
- Improving human resource management systems by using incentives tied to performance indicators.

ICT can be applied to improve the supply of each function or service and at the same time strengthen transparency, accountability, and DFGG. Optimally used, ICT can modernize and reengineer government processes (to make resource management more efficient and responsive, for example), and at the same time render them transparent, enable oversight, and strengthen social accountability. To reduce corruption, information should be more readily available while corruption-prone services should be transferred online.

A second broad area of ICT-enabled governance is *services to citizens*. Improving public service access and quality is a political, social, and economic imperative for all developing countries, and particularly for many African countries that have persistently weak human development indicators and are unlikely to reach Millennium Development Goals on time. One way to improve the availability and quality of public services is to enable citizen monitoring and feedback. This is perhaps the most fertile area for using ICT to strengthen accountability via citizens and social intermediaries, using mobile and e-government service delivery. Applications in Africa have ranged from managing water supply, land titles, licenses, permits, and certificates via citizen-centric portals and community access centers, to the delivery and monitoring of health and education services, to providing choice and competition in service delivery through information brokerage and the use of PPPs.

A third area is to *enhance transparency and reduce the costs of government-to-business transactions*, support entrepreneurship and small enterprise development, and facilitate trade. This is a crucial area for Africa's future with its potential for employment generation, competitiveness, and broad-based growth. These functions are enabled by e-government and mobile applications. Relevant transactions and services cover customs, public procurement, online business registration, access to land records, municipal services to business, financial services (including mobile-based transactions), monitoring of agricultural and other extension services, and monitoring government regulations enforcement. Although there are promising grassroots innovations in this area, they lag behind ICT applications in their support of government accountability in service provision. This is perhaps due to conflicting interests and weak partnerships among business intermediaries, development partners, and NGOs.

Another area for leveraging ICT for governance is to *enhance the effectiveness and accountability of political, oversight, and policy institutions*; enforce the rule of law; and modernize the legislative and judicial branches of government. For example, ICT can improve parliamentary processes through enhancing transparency and openness, providing information to citizens; improving legislative accountability mechanisms; enabling intra-parliamentary and citizen dialogue; and helping citizens keep an eye on Parliament. Other examples include monitoring elections and crowdsourcing data from citizens on violence, human rights abuses, and crisis situations, and enhancing the capacity and transparency of policymaking and oversight institutions.

Governance and Country Context

Through various engagements with country clients, I increasingly realized the importance of placing the various digital governance technologies and applications into a broader social, political, institutional, informational, and stakeholder context. Success in digital government reforms is heavily dependent on in-depth understanding of local context. Service providers and consumers can benefit from information flows that enable consumers to provide feedback on the quality of service, and providers to offer better services, provided incentives are aligned with this objective. A range of state and nonstate actors can be involved in strengthening DFGG that gains momentum when driven by a reform coalition. My research suggests that the context also determines the impact of technologies which calls for understanding the incentives, capabilities, and strategies of the stakeholders, and the institutional and sociopolitical contexts within which a technological intervention is meant to increase accountability.

I explored the various entry levels open to ICT interventions and measures to mobilize the appropriate stakeholders and coalitions at the local, sectoral, national, regional, and/or global levels to demand good governance. Increasingly, I realized the Bank and other major financing institutions should enter at the sector or national-level to secure scalability and sustainability, and to complement and reinforce the efforts of civil society organizations and social intermediaries. A holistic, country-level approach that would nurture national ecosystems and remedy many of the factors that undermine the sustainability of ICT for governance interventions is a must.

Promoting Open and Responsive Government

I have been following and promoting digital transformation of government and public services in both developed and developing countries. I confess I am not an expert in designing or deploying the complex technologies and software systems that enable such transformation: keeping abreast of technological change and the corresponding opportunities and risks is a marathon for development practitioners. Still, this challenge was part of my attraction to this new development practice. My interest in modernizing public management and decision-making helped me understand the changing context in which digital transformation takes place and drove me to promote government-wide strategies and complementary policies, incentives, and skills needed to manage the transformation process. My research and experience in digital government are documented in several books and articles reflecting the fast evolution of this field and my learnings over the last two decades (Hanna 2008, 2010, 2012a, 2016, 2017).

Digitization of public administration has been taking place since the 1980s. It remains a long journey with many associated pitfalls and risks. The Bank and other aid agencies have been increasingly engaged in assisting countries on this journey, but not taking a leading role. At the Bank, assistance was often driven by a few technology specialists unsupported by senior management or corporate strategy. For most of the 1980s–1990s, it was limited to ICT application components in traditional public sector projects. With time, these applications grew in complexity to address strategic public systems such as tax administration and revenue management, public finance and expenditure, public procurement, civil service information management, and so on. These applications required technical skills that were in short supply in both the public service and aid agencies.

In the mid-1990s, with the spread of the Internet and mobile phones, digital government began to address online delivery of basic public services combined with business-process-reengineering and the simplification and integration of government processes. As digital technologies developed, digital transformation projects grew in complexity, requiring public–private partnerships and change management skills. Whole-of-government approaches became necessary. Digital platforms like cloud computing and unique digital identification were introduced—adding more inclusion, flexibility, and resilience. Industrialized countries raced to offer more online services to their citizens and businesses. Some small and newly independent countries like Estonia leapfrogged ahead of many industrialized countries. Many public services were co-created by networks of government-business-NGO collaborators.

Much of this progress, however, was in high-income countries and regions where demand for better services and accountable government was taken for granted. Specialized skills, data privacy protection, cybersecurity, and other ingredients of a healthy digital transformation ecosystem were put in place and continuously upgraded. This was not the case for most developing countries. It is in this context that mobilizing demand for good government was born. It was a new chapter of my journey.

Challenges for Open Government

First of all, it is important to better understand the sociopolitical context and address the motivations of stakeholders. An accurate diagnosis of context and theory of change is critical to the success of technology for transparency interventions. Policymakers and project designers should address all state-citizen-service provider interactions and think through the implications of proposed interventions for all involved.

Secondly, it is important to build local partnerships and local capacity to adopt participatory practices. Effective deployment of ICT for governance and service delivery calls for partnership among government policymakers, regulators, network operators, and service providers; hardware manufacturers and content providers; application developers; civil society organizations (CSOs); and development partners. CSOs' insufficient capacity to meaningfully participate in accountability mechanisms was clear in many cases in Africa, thus the importance of developing CSOs' capabilities. To build CSO partnerships and capacity the Bank should engage with a broader range of stakeholders and reach out to those already active in DFGG.

Partnerships should also be practiced within the Bank, to bridge the disciplinary gaps between ICT specialists, poverty reduction economists, public sector experts, social development, and sector staff. Collaborating with other major development partners is also critical in an area where many potential partners have been working at the community level and perhaps have more intimate knowledge of the local context than the big aid agencies.

Thirdly, it is critical for both ICT and governance practitioners to choose the appropriate entry level for their interventions and mobilize the necessary stakeholders and coalitions at the selected entry level. So far, the standalone digital governance project or its ICT component has been the primary entry level. National-level entry points are critical for attaining large-scale and sustainable impact, and securing the necessary enabling environment for successful ICT interventions. Policy work at the country level may be also necessary to assess the enabling environment for civic engagement and for ICT interventions—for example, freedom of information laws; open government and open budget initiatives; NGO regulation; strengthening the media, judiciary, and independent accountability institutions; and so on.

Fourth, it is necessary to secure political commitment and develop leadership competencies. Building leadership and grassroots awareness and competencies is critical to leverage ICT as an integral part of improving governance and strengthening DFGG. Public sector leaders and chief information officers should develop the competencies to promote open government, manage information resources and open data systems, engage citizens and leverage social networks, and hone the competencies needed to integrate knowledge and skills from multiple participants, including social intermediaries. This should be combined with programs to heighten political leaders' awareness of the opportunities inherent in mobilizing the demand and supply of technology for governance. E-leaders should be developed within and outside of government to lead the transformation to open development and open institutions.

Fifth, it is important to develop government capacity for digital transformation—both institutional and human. Institutional coordination across government to secure shared platforms and a whole-of-government approach is no simple task, as I learnt in Sri Lanka and India. Who should take the lead? How can leadership induce both compliance and collaboration among the transforming agencies? Capacity building in the public sector is a serious challenge in developing countries where almost all capacity-building activities are funded and designed by donor agencies. Moreover, such programs are often not adapted or tested in the individual country context. Given high civil service turnover due to corruption, poor compensation, and unfair recognition, donor investments in capacity building tend to be unsustainable and ineffective. In countries where digital skills are scarce and civil service compensation lags far behind the private sector, capacity for digital government transformation must be continuously rebuilt.

Sixth, scaling and sustaining pilot project successes requires an *appropriate balance* between demonstrating quick results in the short term, and taking a long-term perspective to ensure sustainability and impact. Decentralization, democratization, and public sector reforms involve many long-term measures. Short-term measures include developing information systems that enhance transparency, opening government databases to external actors, and exploiting platforms such as mobile phones, crowdsourcing, and social media. Long-term strategies should lay the foundations to expand, sustain, and deepen short-term measures—through improving the enabling environment, mobilizing constituencies for sustain improvement, building on existing NGO and government social accountability strategies, and aligning initiatives to long-term objectives. From an NGO perspective, funders should focus *on ICT interventions that are replicable elsewhere.* From a large aid agency perspective, incremental innovations should be complemented by long-term measures for scaling and sustainability.

Seventh, the government, the Bank, and other players should be focused on the functioning of the overall ecosystem as it impacts both technology and governance. They should promote ecosystems that support mobile phone and SME networks, social media, startups, and interactive mapping technologies. They should help governments overcome silos by developing data sharing policies and common digital platforms for the whole government. They should support partnerships among NGOs/CSOs, content providers, software developers, mobile operators, and government/service providers to improve the overall functioning of the digital transformation ecosystem as it impacts public governance.

Eighth, e-government strategies should combine supply and demand measures, and aim to improve the supply of services, while crafting information and communication systems that deepen transparency and accountability. Applying ICT to strengthen the supply of services and DFGG should be done synergistically for maximum impact on governance and public service delivery. Different stages of e-government and governance may call for different sequencing strategies. Strengthening supply capacity through e-government programs takes more time to implement than that needed for simple mobile-based applications to strengthen accountability. Some mobile-based DFGG applications can be successfully deployed under the least developed conditions and—to a certain extent—even in the absence of commensurate progress on the supply side. But ultimately, the promise associated with the fast diffusion of mobile and social networks as tools for demand-driven governance may be false or short lived, if digital transformation and a culture of openness in public service are not advanced in tandem. Mobilizing DFGG without building commensurate response capacity and change management risks popular discontent.

Ninth, pro-poor policies should be systematically integrated into ICT for governance. Current digital and participatory divides should not be allowed to distort the outcomes of social accountability mechanisms or accountability to the poor as beneficiaries of public services. Priority should be given to diagnosing the enabling environment and sociopolitical context for pro-poor governance—to address issues such as media coverage, and capture the voices of poor citizens and their social intermediaries through various DFGG tools. Measures include mobilizing, raising awareness, building capacity, and engaging pro-poor forums and social intermediaries to ensure that DFGG mechanisms truly reflect the voices and priorities of the poor. It also means embedding transparency and accountability to beneficiaries into poverty reduction programs. Elements of the ICT ecosystem can be developed to bridge the digital divide and strengthen pro-poor governance: measures to facilitate access to technologies for the poor, for example, community services centers, mobile applications, open-source solutions, local content, liberal licensing of community radio, and building the capacity of social intermediaries (SIs) to promote informational capabilities and ICT literacy.

My final recommendation is to engage in systematic learning. Digital transformation of government is a long learning journey. Although successful examples exist, the "how" of social accountability and the most effective use of ICT for DFGG are still to be explored. Research, systematic learning-by-doing, and the sharing of best practices are urgently needed. National "challenge funds" may be created to experiment and learn from innovative use of ICT for DFGG. Monitoring and evaluation should go beyond a few celebrated successes. Much of the required learning has to be at the local, national, and regional levels through networks and communities of practice. Systematic learning would involve communities, implementation partners, and funders.

Concluding

My experience in developing countries suggests that the most critical challenges to realizing the potential of the new digital technologies for social accountability and governance are political and institutional. These include a shallow understanding of sociopolitical context; weak enabling policies and institutions; low political commitment; limited capacity of CSOs to scale and secure sustainability; weak partnerships among local stakeholders; and disciplinary blinders and turf barriers among specialists concerned with technology, governance, social development, and service sectors.

Large aid agencies should consider whether intervening at the project or micro level is faster, more results-oriented, better focused on specific service delivery, and closer to citizens' needs, or if moving to the sectoral or national level is needed to strategically address national policies and government-wide transformation ecosystems. Offering online public services without first addressing the underlying whole-of-government ecosystem would amount to "window dressing." On balance, I think aid agencies like the Bank should systematically move to the higher plane and address the policy and institutional foundations of the whole ecosystem to secure scale and sustainability. Such high-level interventions may be best complemented by CSOs' targeted assistance and innovations at the pilot or single application level.

While far from perfect, Kenya is an example of a promising national ICT ecosystem for strengthening DFGG.

The Kenya Case

The open government data movement has been catching up—even in low-income countries in Africa—to capture moments of transformational political change. On July 8, 2011, President Mwai Kibaki launched the Kenyan Open Data Initiative (http://opendata.go.ke) making key government data freely available to the public through a single online portal. The 2009 census data, national and regional expenditures, and information on key public services were among the first data sets to be released. Tools and applications have already been developed to process these data. This, so far, is largely the story of open government data in many countries. The box below outlines several distinguishing features of Kenya's open government data initiative.

The open data initiative in Kenya was special: it came at a time of political change, it had a head start on tools and expertise from the global open data community, and it happened in a country where the information ecosystem was still maturing.

First, this initiative arrived just as a new constitution was being adopted by the country. First of all, its launch coincided with the adoption of this initiative arrived just as a new constitution was being adopted by the country. This was an opportunity to affirm the practice and principles of open government at a time of national change, when the local developer community was eager to make use of data, and the public wanted to promote transparency and accountability.

Secondly, the understanding and expectations of open data were maturing. The data.gov of the US government was closely followed by the data.gov.uk and some of the 22 other international open government data sites around the world (as of 2012). Practitioners of open data had started to figure out what works, what doesn't, and why. Kenya's open data initiative had already benefitted from the successes and failures of others, and had connected with the global open data community.

Finally, Kenya was the first low-income country to have an open government data portal. This brought into focus the supply and demand sides of government information that other countries took for granted.

The call for open data should go hand in hand with a call for better-quality data: data that may be collected by official government agencies or—in this age—by citizens themselves.

On the demand side, there was a desire for more information. People wanted the same data as anywhere else in the developed world: land registry, company registrations, employment statistics, to name a few. Kenyans also wanted data that citizens of developed countries were less likely to ask for: information on fire protection (number of fire engines per county), government funds transfers to schools (do they actually reach schools?), and livestock populations.

Kenya is also an example of a relatively developed ecosystem for both DFGG and ICT in Africa. It is not by accident that many innovative ICT governance applications came from Kenya. Several factors contribute to the relatively advanced state of the DFGG and ICT ecosystems. Kenya hosts a disproportionate concentration of international NGOs partly because it offers access to Somalia, Ethiopia, Eritrea, Sudan, Rwanda, and Burundi and partly because of its Cold War importance as a perceived democracy in the region. Given its relatively advanced and vibrant ICT ecosystem, Kenya can make full use of its ICT capacity for combined supply and demand measures for good governance.

Building effective social accountability requires action on the supply side to create an enabling legal-regulatory-institutional framework for bottom-up accountability, and on the demand side, to build the capacity of citizens, communities, and Civil Society Organizations (CSOs) to engage effectively. Strengthening these mechanisms is important for maintaining momentum on the governance agenda in Kenya.

A holistic, country-level approach to digital technology for governance must further nurture these ecosystems and remedy many of the factors that undermine ICT for DFGG interventions. Adopting a more strategic and effective approach to social accountability across the Bank's Kenya portfolio and perhaps across the overall development strategy of Kenya would address key structural factors influencing the ecosystems for DFGG and the supporting DFGG and ICT ecosystems. for DFGG and the supporting ICT ecosystems. A holistic approach to develop these ecosystems further may strengthen the application of social accountability tools in community-driven development projects to improve service delivery to poor and marginalized communities. It may also support the inclusion of appropriate social accountability rules and mechanisms in the legal, regulatory, and institutional frameworks for decentralization and public financial management. A holistic approach would also support innovative applications of ICT for social accountability to expand information dissemination and strengthen citizen feedback opportunities. Finally, it may encourage knowledge and experience sharing among stakeholders engaged in social accountability in Kenya and build South-South partnerships and links with regional practitioners.

CHAPTER 5

Transforming Sectors: The Health Case

Abstract This chapter uses the example of e-Health for sector-wide transformation. It covers the key components of the e-Health system and the challenges to greater uptake of e-Health. National e-Health strategies are examined. The chapter concluded with a vision of creating a health learning system. Progress toward this vision will require better understanding of the health ecosystem and barriers to change—political, institutional, policies, incentives, skills, and digital capabilities. This understanding of the ecosystem and enabling conditions should help inform a research agenda and policy action to ensure that the emerging smart healthcare models are accepted and timely used with maximum benefits for all stakeholders.

Keywords Digital health · e-Health system · National healthcare strategy · Health learning ecosystem · Capabilities

I select the health sector as example of sector-wide digital transformation, cutting across public and private services and linking bottom-up applications with sector-wide policies and digital capabilities. Countries, regions, or cities may choose to focus on transforming one or more sectors, harvesting quick wins, learning to scale, and/or addressing priority needs. My experiences and those of Bank colleagues in many countries suggest

N. K. Hanna, *Driving Digital Transformation in Developing Nations*, https://doi.org/10.1007/978-3-031-54573-3_5

that a sector focus can be used first as beachhead from which to drive wider digital transformation to other sectors, for a country, region, or city.[1]

Many factors that drive sector transformation are not fundamentally different from those required for transforming government. Basic among them are a shared vision of the future; support to sector policy reforms; readiness for e-transformation; investing in sector-wide digital platforms, continuous assessment of performance and service delivery; and systematic dealing with the gaps in the digital ecosystem of the target sector.

It is a common pitfall to commit to ICT investments that are not in sync with the sector's reform strategy and thus ignore the incentive system and the needed investment in complementary skills and organizational changes. A second pitfall is to view ICT as a short-term technological enhancement, rather than a deep socio-technical transformation. A third is to proceed with major ICT investments without a shared vision for the future. A fourth is to excessively rely on a single ICT tool (often the latest fad or the next new thing) without deploying other elements of the ecosystem. All of these are avoidable, but frequent in practice, leading to high levels of failure in meeting transformational objectives. Alternatively, they create islands of innovation and isolated best practices, but fail to diffuse and scale, or lead to sector-wide step change and impact.

To realize the potential of digital transformation, ICT interventions must be guided by a clear vision of the sector, appreciation of current challenges and future opportunities, and substantive sector policy reform. Sector leaders should communicate at all levels a well-articulated shared vision. An energizing vision will motivate key stakeholders to buy-in and change, initiate coherent reforms, facilitate partnerships, mobilize resources for strategic investments in ICT and complementary assets, and commit management to sustained change efforts.

Transformational technology leaders, including CIOs, should engage in this process, to understand the demand side and inform other executives of what is realistically possible with the new technologies, as well as the best practices that can be transferred from other sectors or countries. ICT leaders and target sector leaders must be creatively engaged so that

[1] This section draws on and adapted from Hanna (2016).

the intended reforms for the target sector can drive ICT-enabled transformations. At the same time, ICT leaders can open up possibilities for innovations, new services, and new paths to transformation.

Readiness assessments and benchmarking are useful tools to apply to sector-level transformation, as much as they are useful for transforming government or the whole economy. Assessments should cover sector leadership, political economy of the sector, and incentives and organizational structures needed to support digital transformation. It would also include ICT skills and resources of the sector, existing online services and digital data, and connectivity and shared communication infrastructure. In addition to e-readiness, vision development and transformation priorities of a targeted sector will benefit from comparator indicators of sector performance and outcome, as in comparative costs and levels of health services and educational achievements across countries, and among cities and regions of a country. Such contextual understanding of the sector and its performance challenges is at least as critical as assessing its e-readiness in order to guide transformational priorities.

Transforming Health Services

The health sector requires extensive use of information and communication to make decisions and deliver services. The absence of timely and reliable information contributes to inefficient uses of human, facilities, and financial resources, and ultimately to poor health outcomes. Making health systems more efficient and responsive requires seamless, sustainable, and secure data and information exchanges at all levels of the health system.

The potential for e-Health (including telemedicine and m-health) for service delivery and sector management is huge—for remote diagnosis of patients in India's rural areas; surveillance and alerts for HIV patients in South Africa and the elderly in Chile; tracking drug supply and demand at rural health clinics in Kenya and Malawi; modernizing rural hospital management information systems and electronic records in Sri Lanka; and improving measurement, accountability, and collaboration across the whole health sector.[2] In Peru, a mobile application uses SMS messages to deliver information on health and nutrition during pregnancy. In Kenya,

[2] World Bank, IC4D (2012): Maximizing Mobile (2012).

e-learning has been used for training to upgrade nurses, who otherwise have no access to advanced training.[3] ICT is also used for timely monitoring of the spread of disease and analysis of causes and sources for preventing strategies, as in the spread of malaria in Kenya. In Uganda, maternal mortality dropped by 50% when rural care was provided under the Ultimate Emergency Relief during Pregnancy and Childbirth, using a mix of technologies.

Using ICT to transform the health system can optimize the use of scarce resources and help bridge the urban–rural divide in health care, for example, by leveraging specialist doctors and expensive MRI machines using remote analysis and diagnosis. While m-health applications may have focused on telemonitoring of patients at home in developed countries, they should address problems of access to scarce resources such as doctors and medicine in developing countries. The potential value of widespread use of e-Health in the developing countries is likely to be greater, since it could help maximize the reach and impact of smaller number of highly-trained physicians and clinical staff in rural and remote areas. ICT connectivity opens new options for redesigning health delivery systems that would be less facilities-intensive than traditional ones.

There is growing consensus that any systematic effort to address the challenges facing the health systems all over the world requires intensive use of information and communication (enabled by technology) to support new and smarter service and management models. Alongside these models, a vision for a *learning health system* is emerging, one in which "progress in science, informatics, and care culture align to generate new knowledge as an ongoing, natural by-product of the care experience, and seamlessly refine and deliver best practices for continuous improvement in health and healthcare" (Grossman et al. 2011).

Components of the e-Health System[4]

E-health covers the full range of potential uses of ICT, from health management systems to clinical decision support and patient information and tools, to support to all aspects of communication, measurement, and

[3] Accenture, African Medical and Research Foundation: E-Learning (2005).

[4] This part draws on e-Health Technical Paper, June 2015. Paper submitted to MA4Health conference, on Measurement and Accountability for Results in Health, A Common Agenda for the Post-2015 Era.

accountability for results. These can be summarized in terms of seven broad application areas:

> First category is patient care management systems. These include electronic medical records, hospital information systems, telemedicine, and all other systems that aid clinicians in the diagnosis and treatment of health care for individuals, and which enables the sharing of the clinical information across the continuum of care.
> Second is the population management systems. These are concerned with the health of the population as a whole, including public health information systems and consumer health information system—the latter helps patients manage their own health. They also include the emerging "Big Data" applications which allow us to detect patterns, to formulate hypotheses for clinical research, and to fashion clinical guidelines and protocols.
> Third is disease state management systems. These systems reflect the increasing need to manage chronic diseases, which are costly, and must be managed over long horizons and across levels of care and different venues.
> Fourth is scarce resource management systems. These attempt to track, regulate, monitor, and optimize the supply chains of health care's scarce resources. This primarily involves healthcare workers, and managing their productivity, and continuing professional training and development. These systems also deal with optimizing the supply chain (logistics) for drugs—a major cost item and critical to availability and lifesaving.
> Fifth is utilization management systems. These can measure the degree of productivity of each element of healthcare delivery, optimize the use of health services, and help deliver the right amount of services, at the right place, and at the right time.
> Sixth is financial management systems. These are critical to budgeting, accountability, and resource planning. They include enterprise resource planning systems, which must orchestrate resources with medical care needs. They also support sophisticated health financing schemes, health insurance, provider payments, claim processing, etc.
> Seventh category is quality management systems. They measure quality of medical care overall, and the perceived quality by the patients. Increasing emphasis is on health outcomes. These must

be drawn from accurate, timely, and complete data flowing from the six categories described above. Mobile phone feedback systems present a new opportunity to collect both clinical and population-based quality and timely feedback from end-users of these systems. They are increasingly used even in poor settings to learn about user satisfaction, and enable social monitoring of health programs.

Each of the above application areas plays important roles in measuring and accounting for health results. E-Health strategies must address them all so as to take a holistic view of the sector, its governance and performance, and of the interdependencies and information sharing across these systems.

Challenges to e-Health

The most relevant challenges to the greater uptake of e-Health include:

- Common perception of e-Health as peripheral to health services delivery and management, or a "silver bullet" which requires a single large-scale investment rather than a planned, sequenced, integrated, and continuous approach.
- Fragmented, uncoordinated, short-term funding that is too often focused on standalone pilots and single application.
- Inadequate integration of e-Health financing (payment systems) with rest of healthcare infrastructure.
- Business models not adapted to match the scarcity of resources both on the demand and supply side in the developing world.
- Privacy and security concerns, with limitations on access to patient data that can complicate interaction with the rest of the ecosystem, or weak legal frameworks and practices that undermine trust and privacy.
- Governance to ensure that multiple stakeholders are contributing to e-Health development. E-Health governance covers the processes and standards that enable effective, secure, and timely collection, creation, storage, exchange, and ethical use and protection of health information. It also includes agreed upon shared enterprise architecture and standards to ensure interoperability.

- Collaboration among stakeholders, including private, public, and development agencies for e-Health. In particular, collaboration between the health and ICT sectors, both public and private, is central to e-Health strategic planning.
- Piecemeal implementation of e-Health products and services, which leads to poor interoperability between applications that run on different platforms.
- Limited understanding of the policy environment and technical ecosystem that will be necessary to foster and sustain scaled e-Health solutions at the national level.
- Shortages in human resources for e-Health, particularly in the public sector.
- The impact of e-Health services not regularly assessed.

These challenges must be added to the governance and policy challenges in the health sector more broadly. Reforms in governance, policies, incentives, and human resources within the health sector—the whole ecosystem—must be aligned to support e-Health applications.

National e-Health Strategies

E-Health strategies should build on learning from pilots and experiments that target pressing problems and prevalent diseases in developing countries while demonstrating feasibility and measurable results. They should simultaneously aim for scalability and sustainability, and for strengthening health systems across programs. Such system-wide transformation requires major changes in institutions and individual behavior. It requires understanding and monitoring the behavior of patients and service providers, to devise appropriate incentives for change, and to learn from implementation. It requires frameworks, protocols, and standards to scale up successful pilots and integrate bottom-up initiatives. It also calls for partnerships between public agencies, private sector, and civil society. Above all, it demands transformational leadership and change management.

E-Health strategies should consider the complex ecosystem of health, which they intend to transform and sustain. This means taking into account the incentives and human factors that influence timely and accurate data collection, the culture of data sharing, and the utilization of data in health decision-making. E-Health systems are expected to be interoperable to allow broad integration across multiple and synergistic health information systems. All e-Health applications need to be integrated into the overall healthcare system and strategy.

A governance and regulation perspective is critical. It focuses on the role of government IT officers in implementing the e-Health strategy, but does not explicitly require collaboration between IT practitioners and health practitioners. In all health and other services environments, cross-disciplinary collaboration should be considered the foundation of successful transformative ventures.

The investment, affordability, and sustainability angle raises the necessity of long-term planning and budgeting (perhaps 10 years), in contrast to the historical medium-term budgeting (three-year budgeting). Long-term budgeting can be seen as an important measure for introducing programs that will mature over five years or more.

Capacity and workforce development assigns priority to health informatics professionals as a new practitioner group in the healthcare environment; it calls for collaborative partnerships for training such professionals.

Recent policies of emerging market countries like India have emphasized knowledge management and knowledge networks to support medical research and practice; advanced communication infrastructure; the use of open technologies and standards; drug surveillance; the networking among medical colleges, research institutions, and premier health service providers; partnerships with international organizations; development of EHRs; integrating medical informatics into medical and paramedical curriculum; and developing analytics for healthcare financing, trends predicting, and performance monitoring.

Ecosystem View of Health Sector Transformation

Increasingly, e-Health stakeholders are realizing the need to arrive at a more holistic understanding of the ecosystem not only to base implementation on best practices but also to factor in local circumstances. The large number of different stakeholder groups requires that their different roles and responsibilities be clarified. Because e-Health always exists within and interacts with a country's larger healthcare system (the analog complements), it will be affected by public policy, private sector influence, diverse patient needs, and the interests of several other participants.

Taking an ecosystem view of the sector or context where e-Health is applied should help planners avoid a one-size-fits-all approach. Accordingly, e-Health applications should be designed to respond to people's needs and suited to their local context. A common pitfall is that, once an application is working well technically and is seen to have high potential, there is an immediate tendency to implement it everywhere regardless of context or analog complements. Conducting readiness assessments with users can help avoid such overextension. Close involvement of health practitioners in the design and development of ICT applications and mobile content can ensure fitting the tool to the context.

Pilots have so far pursued specific health problems or targets of opportunities. But e-Health programs should be viewed and aligned within the broader contexts of national health care and e-government programs. Sustainability and scalability of e-Health programs ultimately depend on common platforms or building blocks. The targets of opportunity will vary among developed and developing countries, but an ecosystem's view remains essential for sustainable progress and scalable impact.

Emerging Lessons

Country experiences suggest the following critical success factors to drive e-Health adoption:

- *National leadership to promote e-Health adoption.* Global leaders pursue national-level strategies to drive and coordinate e-Health adoption.
- *Ownership.* Effective country ownership, broad participation of key stakeholders, good governance, and strong human and institutional resources are at the core of e-Health planning and implementation. In turn e-Health solutions can facilitate governance, participation, and human resources development. Engaging the public in building better understanding of e-Health as an enabling technology can broaden ownership and build support for digital transformation.
- *Integration of e-Health with health sector.* E-Health cannot be pursued in silo or parallel to health sector planning. It should be seamlessly integrated with sector policy reforms, and person-centered systems and services.
- *Healthcare system organization and financing.* Costs and benefits of investing in IT systems for health care are better aligned in countries with single-payer healthcare systems. They can also afford to take a longer-term view and make investments that may not pay off in the

short term (this presents a challenge for larger countries with diverse populations and decentralized supply structure).

- *Common health IT infrastructure.* Creating a shared platform for healthcare organizations to use can lower costs, increase information sharing and interoperability, and accelerate implementation. Sweden has developed a national broadband network for the secure exchange of health information connecting all hospitals, primary care centers, among others; it also used this infrastructure for video conferencing, teleradiology, and e-learning in medical schools.
- *User-centered healthcare systems.* The systems should leverage the capacity of citizens to contribute information and feedback. Leveraging ICT platforms, including mobile, Web, social media, and SMS, and accessing personal data in EHRs can enhance accountability, transparency, and empowerment of citizens. Access to mobile health approaches and tools, and broadband content should also support improved decision-making by frontline providers.
- *Use of unique patient identifiers.* UID helps facilitate data sharing between healthcare organizations. Benefits include reduced risk of medical error, improved efficiency, and better privacy protection for patients.
- *Government policies* and mandates are essential to spur e-Health, such as making e-prescribing mandatory for primary care providers, addressing privacy issues, and facilitating standard setting processes.
- *Innovation and adaptation.* It is important to recognize the diversity of solutions of e-Health, as certain countries may be ready for particular e-Health solutions, while others may require the development of missing ecosystems prior to going to scale. E-Health opens up new possibilities for innovation in measurement, data collection from the point of care, management systems, collaboration, accountability, patient engagement, capacity building, adaptation, and learning. So, creating supportive and virtuous ecosystems for bottom-up innovation and adaptation will be critical to digital transformation of health systems.

National government policies can play an important role in shaping and facilitating a country's adoption of e-Health and its effective use to transform the whole system. Investing in e-Health must be guided by such national policies to lead to scalable and sustainable change.

A Health Learning System

The journey toward a future health learning system will be fueled by the transformative power of digitization and connectivity. For OECD countries, the emerging vision is of a learning health system, based on real-time and personalized information. Realizing this vision will require enhanced capacity to share, process, and analyze large streams of data from heterogeneous sources and a major change from traditional practices. A transformed healthcare system will need to be proactive, preventive, and focused on quality of life. The new system would shift from hospital/doctor-centered to community/patient-centered. Data would be generated and aggregated from digital clinical and administrative records, advances in genomics, new diagnostics and medical imaging, sensor and mobile technologies, and geospatial location tools. These data must be captured, harmonized, and converted into meaningful information at all levels, and particularly at the point of care. This should generate system-wide efficiencies, including for healthcare diagnostics, delivery, research, and innovation.

With the fast declining cost of having a personal human genome map, it is possible to envision a future in which treatments are tailored to individuals' genetic structures, prescriptions are analyzed in advance for likely effectiveness, and researchers study clinical data in real time to learn what works. With this personalized medicine, treatments are better targeted, therapies not likely to be effective for particular people are avoided, and researchers and health administrators have a better understanding of comparative effectiveness.

Progress toward this vision will require better understanding of the health ecosystem and barriers to change—political, institutional, policies, incentives, skills, and digital capabilities. This understanding of the ecosystem and enabling conditions should help inform a research agenda and policy action to ensure that the emerging smart healthcare models are accepted and timely used with maximum benefits for all stakeholders. It should address the challenges of personalized medicine, the new privacy and security risks, incentives for radical and social innovation, and incentives to various actors with different organizational cultures and roles. It is also necessary to understand the regulatory structures that provide incentives at different levels of the health ecosystem to encourage investments in new models of health care.

Progress also requires moving from silos of technology toward an integrated ecosystem of smart solutions. New smart models of care are increasingly being shaped by convergent technologies. Barriers to such convergence should be addressed to secure integration and interoperability. There will be also a huge need for training health providers and community health workers in the use of the new technology platforms, and for improving patient understanding and use of these new tools.

Health system transformation demands research. Research should address challenges to data integrity and develop robust procedures for aggregation and analysis. New risks should be anticipated, including unintended outcomes. Attention should be given to quality assurance, monitoring of use, identification of potential adverse outcomes or intentional abuses, timely analysis of incidents, and creation of appropriate regulation.

For developing countries, this vision requires local experimentation and adaptation in search of frugal and inclusive innovations. This may mean, among others, more emphasis on telemedicine, access to medical information and diagnosis via kiosks and clinics in schools and markets, and making hospitals more of a network, less of a big box with all specialists co-located. Mobile technology confers eyes, ears, voice, reach, and knowledge. It will educate patients about aliments and symptoms via websites, and mothers about nutrition and baby care. Small test centers can spread across areas currently devoid of modern medicine. Developing countries will have to build the system from the ground up, with local adaptation and experimentation to overcome last-mile problem of health service delivery, and empower local health providers with information and patients with choice. Such a health system will also need to give attention to mapping and monitoring the devastating and endemic diseases like malaria, TB, and Covid-19. It should capture a lot more real-time information from the field to spin the learning cycle faster.

CHAPTER 6

Transforming Cities: Smart Cities

Abstract In view of growing urbanization and concerns about climate change, can smart city applications help city leaders and stakeholders manage these challenges in spite of turf rivalries? Cities in the developing world are facing unprecedented challenges and opportunities in an increasingly urbanized, connected, and digitally-empowered environment.

Keywords Smart city definition · Smart city applications · Rio case · China's smart city program · India's smart city

In 2016, a challenging opportunity came up unexpectedly. I would be helping WBG's urban practice define a path to integrate smart city solutions into urban development. There was much hype about the way new digital technologies were transforming cities in both developed and developing countries.

I started my career at the Bank with an assignment in urban development. Visiting Jakarta, Indonesia, back in 1975–1976, I saw the challenges of rapid urbanization first-hand, as villages surrounding Jakarta were integrated into a densely populated Jakarta center. There was clear tension between addressing the pressing needs of these slums and

N. K. Hanna, *Driving Digital Transformation in Developing Nations*,
https://doi.org/10.1007/978-3-031-54573-3_6

investing in Jakarta's underdeveloped transport, water and sewage infrastructure. It was a tension between long-term environmental and urban growth management, on the one hand, and immediate demand for basic urban services—on the other hand. I have lived in many cities, starting with Cairo, and observed the fast rise of other cities like Singapore and felt that urbanization challenges and opportunities in the developing world could not be greater.

In 2016, the Bank's urban management department asked me whether we could have smart cities without smart ICT infrastructure or whether we first had to address the underdeveloped physical infrastructures of developing cities? Any possible solutions that would integrate the traditional and digital infrastructures of cities? I could not resist the offer to examine the urban development practice through the new lens of digital and data technology solutions for cities.

A Changing Environment for Cities

Cities in the developing world face unprecedented challenges and opportunities in an increasingly urbanized, connected, and digitally-empowered world. Daunting city challenges span infrastructure and services gaps, fast-growing populations, slums, environmental and pollution problems, safe-water scarcity, rising inequality, congestion, crime, fragility, financial constraints, and poor urban management systems. Cities also offer much hope as high productivity, innovation and low-cost service delivery centers that encourage decentralization and citizen participation, attract talent and knowledge industries, generate data, create platforms and serve as testbeds for disruptive technologies.

The Internet, smartphones, and data management tools can help to address city challenges and create new paths for urban development. Of the two waves digital technologies—the first bringing computerization and basic digital connectivity, while the second introducing big data, analytics, artificial intelligence, and the Internet of Things (IoT)—smart cities rode the second. Both waves interact in a complex and growing ecosystem that rests on access to digital platforms and computing services.

The integration of digital technologies into city systems and services takes many forms and serves many functions. It improves efficiencies in existing urban systems through the monitoring of real-time data and the use of intelligent systems. Digital technologies transform financial services, smart mobility, and smart energy systems. They can help cities optimize the use of water, electricity, and other infrastructures and thus contribute to resilience and environmental sustainability. The emerging digital ecosystem and its rapid integration into city systems require local capacity to experiment, adapt and innovate.

Defining Smart Cities

Initially, there was a controversy at the Bank regarding the proper definition of a smart city. Different definitions emphasize different smart city elements, but all focus on harnessing data and digital technologies for city development. In my own research, I studied examples of smart city initiatives from all over the world and was impressed by their diversity. Yet, one way or another, they were all focused on building *efficient, innovative, inclusive,* and *resilient cities.*[1]

After interviewing the Bank's global practice staff, I proposed the following consensus-based definition; a smart city is a city that adopts an integrated, cross-sectoral and spatially coordinated approach to the planning and management of city land and property assets, infrastructure, and services. It engages its citizens in the process. It is a city that harnesses the most effective digital technologies and data to enable the achievement of urban development targets. Its leaders make smart decisions in the prioritization of investments and the management of city systems. Smart cities integrate the digital and urban (analog) ecosystems for smart solutions. They can combine top-down approaches and shared platforms of instrumented and digital infrastructures with bottom-up experimentation and innovation by connected and data-empowered citizens.

Why was it critical to get the smart city definition right? Digital technology specialists and major suppliers of digital solutions like IBM and Cisco were excited about the new digital tools and their promise of creating and managing smart cities. For the urban development practitioners in the developing world, the physical infrastructure and utilities were pressing challenges that could not be ignored in favor of digital solutions originally designed for the well-established cities of the industrial world. To many of my urban development colleagues at the Bank, smart city tools appeared to be solutions for ill-defined problems.

[1] Nagy Hanna. 2017. *Smart Cities: How Can the World Bank Help Cities Become Smarter?* World Bank White Paper.

For developing cities, and the Bank practice in particular, the "smart city" label should be interpreted in a context-sensitive way to reflect the realities of cities at distinct levels of development. It would make little sense for a city to use the most advanced digital technologies while neglecting its physical infrastructures and operational management. In some cases, digital solutions can optimize the use of a constrained physical infrastructure, as in the case of intelligent traffic systems to reduce congestion. They can also be part of the solution to scarce planning and weak managerial capabilities that can be augmented with advanced information, financial management, and citizen communication and feedback systems.

For many fast-growing African and South Asian cities, the deficit in physical infrastructure, management systems, and even in basic connectivity must be addressed earlier or together with investments in instrumentation, networks, analytics, and artificial intelligence capabilities. Smart city solutions must build on sound physical infrastructure, strengthened institutions, and other investments in analog complements.

Demand for Smart City Assistance

A Bank sample survey of Task Team Leaders with interest in smart cities suggested areas of high interest were governance, digital connectivity, analytics, smart mobility and transport, and urban planning and management. Another survey of citizens and enterprises of 12 cities in developed and middle-income countries indicated a growing interest of city inhabitants in shaping the services and cities they live in. Like citizens, businesses called for more transparency, more channels of communications, and more engagement of businesses in public decision-making on improving city infrastructure and services.

The Bank created an urbanization policy framework in which planning was given foremost importance, promoting the coordination of land use with infrastructure, especially transport, natural resources, and hazard risk. The framework encourages the tapping of all resources and assets in a city—built assets, contextual advantages, natural features, natural and built heritage—for economic development. Improving the regulatory and financial apparatus in the city would enable such integrated planning and management.

In 2017–2018, I authored a "white" paper providing a brief overview of what the Bank was working on in several promising and innovative smart city engagements. At the time, the Bank had not yet articulated a framework or strategy for smart cites or the role of digital technologies in implementing urbanization policies. The Bank's task leaders were left on their own to decide whether and how to leverage digital technologies for developing cities. They were armed mainly with their own curiosity and willingness to learn. A trust fund supported by the Korean government was used to expose urban specialists to "smart city tools" via seminars and trips to Korea. My paper was also financed from this source. It was not until later that the Bank's top management expressed interest in assisting cities to harness transformative technologies for accelerated development.

I was impressed by the rapidly growing scope of digital technology applications that could be harnessed to deliver smart solutions to cities, and the excitement these generated among city mayors. In many developing countries, including China, Brazil, and India, advanced broadband infrastructures are an integral part of national strategies for smart cities. These are pursued through innovative sharing of infrastructure development (such as electricity, water supply, roads, etc.) and through partnerships between central and local governments, and the private sector. In fact, infrastructure sharing can generate major cost savings—up to 95% of investment in broadband when combined with road construction, for example. Where affordable, community-owned broadband may be one of the best investments a smart city can make.

Smart digital infrastructure provides a foundation for other infrastructures and smart city services. Smart transport and smart mobility involve various approaches that reduce congestion and foster responsive, environmentally-friendly and low-cost options including both—mass transit systems and individual mobility such as on-demand transportation and ride and asset sharing. Intelligent transportation systems connect the entire array of multimodal transport options in a city. They integrate live data from various sources: sensor networks, GPS, dynamic traffic lights, connected cars, navigational systems, etc.

Smart water solutions address the challenge of solving water scarcity problems with innovative technologies and data-based water management. A smart water management system uses digital technologies to help save water, detect leakages in real time, reduce costs, and increase the reliability and transparency of water distribution. Metering the water supply system in Mumbai, for example, led to a 50% reduction in water leakage (Polson 2013).

The integration of digital technologies into city systems and services takes many forms and functions: improving efficiencies in existing urban systems through the monitoring of real-time data and the use of intelligent systems as in smart metering for electricity and water; improving responsiveness as in traffic control and smart public services; improving responsiveness to national disasters and enabling rapid and smart city planning with the use of real-time data from all sources (big data); and applying analytics and artificial intelligence. This integration is also likely to transform many functions: financial services; smart mobility and sharing (Uber); and distributed generation from solar panels that reduces reliance on existing power generation and distribution systems.

Sensors and IOT offer ways to reduce inefficiencies in waste management, enable monitoring the movement of different kinds of waste, and convert waste into a resource. Smart energy management systems (including smart grid) use various digital technologies to automate, monitor and optimize energy distribution and usage, incorporate distributed renewable generation, and automate demand response. Smart buildings integrate and optimize different physical systems to improve energy efficiency and optimize water use. These are estimated to save 30% of water, 40% of energy, and reduce building maintenance costs by 10–30% (Honeywell et al. 2015). And the list goes on to all kinds of smart city services, such as e-government, e-Health, and e-education. Underlying all smart solutions are healthy digital ecosystems and smart infrastructure.

Challenges, Gaps, and Risks

My review showed that developing cities faced several challenges to becoming smarter: weak governance and leadership to build local consensus on smart city initiatives; underdeveloped local capacity to plan and implement smart city initiatives; lack of coordination between municipal silos dealing with cross-cutting change issues; lack of alignment of policies and strategies at various levels of government, inadequate finance and public-private partnerships; limited inclusion of stakeholders in planning and implementation; and inadequate processes and skills for assessing, procuring and localizing digital technologies.

I suggested that the Bank should also address its own challenges: owning the smart city agenda at the country department and global urban practice levels; collaborating among global practices (particularly among urban, transport and digital development practices); partnering with the private sector and civic society organizations; revamping procurement and other assistance tools for agility; and developing cutting-edge skills to match technological demands and help clients adapt smart technology solutions to varying developing cities' contexts.

I concluded that ignoring the smart city movement and emerging lessons from the pioneers is not an option. Yet, smart cities are neither a panacea for all urban problems nor a short-cut to its sustainable development goals. In fact, they come with significant risks, including distorting city development priorities; disconnecting major ICT investments from urban development strategies and analog foundations; adopting technological determinism (ignoring the analog complements); mis-procuring complex systems; replicating current silos from analog to digitized processes; automating existing city government processes and relationships without reforming or redesigning them; increasing vulnerability to cyberattacks causing cascade failures of strategic systems; increasing surveillance and threats to privacy; introducing algorithmic bias as in predictive policing and in delivering services to different groups; and alienating citizens by adopting top-down technocratic approaches.

The Bank also faces significant risks in adopting smart city approaches, including reputational risks arising from its departure from its traditional comparative advantage; undue influence of major tech giants and consulting firms undermining the Bank's role as an honest broker; and the growing incidence of major systems procurement issues, among others. The root cause of these and other risks is inadequate Bank knowledge, skills, processes, and risk management systems to deal with the challenges of the digital revolution and to help client cities work with the private sector to meet city-defined needs and objectives.

The opportunities and challenges facing cities call for governments and development agencies to take a proactive posture toward adopting smart city approaches, and managing the risks inherent in fast and disruptive digital transformation. A proactive posture would harness the enthusiasm of countries and city leaders and the interest of the private sector to enact policy reforms and mobilize investments and partnerships. This posture would involve adopting a holistic long-term framework, prioritizing within this framework, and engaging with cities at multiple levels. Risks must be acknowledged and managed to avoid distorting city development priorities or reinforcing the digital and economic divides. Top-down urban development and digital infrastructure strategies must be complemented by bottom-up innovation initiatives to localize and integrate digital technologies and data within the local context and to strengthen the analog complements.

Development experts I interviewed believe their disciplines and practices are undergoing a paradigm shift induced by the new wave of digital technologies. They do not believe this is a passing fad that is irrelevant to their clients. City leaders all over the world are inspired and attracted to what digital technologies can offer to make their city management systems efficient and effective.

A proactive posture that would mainstream smart city solutions into urban practice does not mean having a set of solutions applied uniformly across cities at different levels of economic, physical, and digital development. Leveraging data, communication channels, and other digital tools should be part of the solutions to the challenges and opportunities facing developing cities. But the pace and degree of adoption of these digital capabilities should be adapted to different city contexts and levels of development.

Some digital building blocks (such as broadband and expenditure and revenue management systems) may be necessary for all cities seeking a smarter future. But cities are pursuing diverse smart city visions and they start from different initial conditions. Development practitioners need to be guided by shared principles and good practices about where to start, where to focus beyond the common building blocks, how to phase and sequence, what may constitute quick wins, and how to keep digital solutions open, adaptable, and sustainable. City leaders and development practitioners should be guided by the urgent problems facing their clients, and the opportunities and aspirations of their cities, rather than standard definitions and off-the-shelf solution sets.

I believe aid agencies must align their skills, incentives and processes with cities' demands for smart solutions. Key challenges for the Bank would be bridging silos among all concerned global practices (urban, ICT, transport, energy, governance, water, and environment), partnering with the IFC, engaging in systematic innovation, and adopting a multi-sector, multi-stakeholder, and multi-partnership approach to making cities smarter. This collaboration is essential to build the digital platforms and ecosystems that would enable scalable and sustainable city solutions for twenty-first-century cities. Given the innovation-intensive nature of smart city practice, both aid agencies and cities must build capacity to engage and learn, develop good practices and mainstream the smart city agenda into development.

Urban Management Response?

My paper attempted to capture the views of Bank TTLs engaged in various sectors and aspects of smart cities. It was a first cut at taking stock of what the Bank and its development partners are doing. Given the magnitude of the opportunities and challenges, I recommended that Bank management take concrete steps toward developing a strategy and action plan for integrating smart city solutions into development practice. A first step would be for the global urban practice management to adopt and communicate a holistic definition of smart city that is inclusive of both: best practices in urban planning and management (the analog ecosystem), and the use of digital technologies and data (the digital ecosystem) in support of stakeholders' participation in shaping their city and its services.

I suggested the establishment of a working group of urban and related global practices to formulate detailed recommendations of the measures needed to assist TTLs to take the lead in prioritizing and mainstreaming smart city practices. Urban and digital development GPs would collaborate on a smart city digital assessment toolkit. The Smart City working group would organize workshops to socialize the proposed smart city assessment tools, pilot them in selected cities, and document good practices to ensure close linkages between urbanization reviews and the digital assessment toolkit. Management would also create a Bank-wide, higher-level task force to review existing collaboration across Global Practices, and make recommendations to overcome gaps.

My presentation to Bank staff summed up my findings and recommendations. The room was packed with many people left standing outside! Several peer reviewers made cogent comments mainly endorsing the findings and the need for a concerted and proactive management response. The senior director and the director of the Urban GP were in attendance.

As the meeting proceeded, it became clear that the senior director was expecting me to deliver a ready-made list of digital tools that could be mechanistically used by TTLs to produce smart cities. Rather than discussing the next steps to be taken by management, he quickly concluded the meeting. It was clear he was not interested in hearing about the need for urban staff to collaborate with the Digital Development (DD) staff on advancing smart city practices. He was not happy to be told that management must take the lead in the transformation of the urban practice. At a later one-on-one meeting with the director, he said he would gradually develop his staff's smart city expertise on his own—no need to collaborate with the DD department.

The Rio Case

Rio de Janeiro, Brazil, a city of 13 million, has used smart city solutions to create an Operations Center to integrate data from 32 agencies, develop an integrated risk management system, and enhance safety, resilience, and sustainability. I had visited Rio, met its city leaders, and enjoyed its natural beauty, but was saddened by the poverty of the favelas and the stark contrast between the rich and the poor. At the time, in 2016, Rio was hailed as a smart city success by IBM and leading technology consultants. Rio's Operations Center was seen as an effective tool to monitor, analyze, and predict weather conditions and coordinate across many city agencies. It was also expected to analyze data to better manage future natural disasters.

Extreme events of the past few years have produced a record number of negative impacts on the population of Rio de Janeiro, displacing thousands and killing hundreds of people. The city might have to endure an increase of up to 3.4 degrees Celsius in average temperatures over the next 65 years, and in 2080 the sea level could rise between 37 and 82 cm. The city is focused on the five priorities set out in the Kyoto Protocol (make disaster reduction a priority; know the risk and take action; build understanding and awareness; reduce risks; and be prepared and ready to act) and has promoted actions that meet these requirements, such as investing in a weather radar and a rain gauge network installed in mobile phone towers to help Civil Defense monitor rainfall.

The Mayor of Rio requested IBM to design an Operations Center of the City of Rio integrating data from 30 agencies (COR). Civil Defense is one of the agencies integrated into the Rio de Janeiro Operations Center (COR-Rio), which also has a landslide prevention system fed with data collected by sensors installed in hazardous slope areas mapped by Geo-Rio. COR-Rio is able to issue alerts with extremely high precision and anticipate storms, floods, and landslides. By relying on the monitoring camera system, it also coordinates the action of the relevant agencies in cases of flooding and obstruction of public streets. One of the main vectors of this integrated emergency response system is interaction with society. By SMS, the web, or social networks the government keeps the public informed in times of crisis. In addition, a siren alarm system was installed in residential communities in high-risk areas.

Evidence suggests that the organized and unorganized parts of the city have different access to services; the militia has its own network and has authority over a large part (about 30 percent) of city management. The organized part is an efficient smart city but the unorganized part functions as an independent entity, disconnected from official city services. Thus, an inclusive city vision will take time and effort beyond technology implementation alone.

It is now clear that data capturing and aggregation and co-location of sectors alone do not solve existing sectoral planning problems that have led to inefficiencies and divided the city. The Operations Center is only an initial step in a long process of applying digital solutions to minimize disruptions and increase Rio's resilience. Digital tools do not substitute for complementary analog factors and capabilities such as sound land use planning, transparent and accountable city governance, local institutional capacity, analytic capabilities, healthy business environment, and social and income inclusion.

Rio smart city is one example of many in the global smart city movement. I consulted several other countries and cities including Jordan, Sri Lanka, India, Singapore, and Dubai that have inspired many other cities. Sri Lanka's Colombo developed a very ambitious land reclamation project supported by Chinese loans. Egypt, among others, felt creating new smart cities was much more attractive than facing endemic infrastructure, utility, and urban congestion problems.

In developed countries, however, there has been some push-back against smart cities over residents' concerns that city governments partnering with big tech companies may lead to unauthorized data collection threatening privacy and security. Without trust between city residents and smart city planners technological progress is likely to halt. Smart city initiatives should be demand driven. They call for building capabilities among stakeholders, both within city administration and among potential beneficiaries. While tech companies, authorities, and city planners are all quick to praise the benefits of smart city initiatives, critics warn many citizens are woefully unprepared or unaware of the impact that data collection systems could have on personal privacy.

This is a development dilemma that must be navigated by societies, governments, and aid agencies. At the Bank, I saw this play out when I was involved with the urban development management department skeptical about smart city solutions, while trying to effectively engage the digital development department that believed digital technologies alone could make cities smarter. My attempts to bridge the gap between these two camps were more successful at the conceptual and staff levels, but less so at the practice and senior directors' levels.

China's Smart City Program

In October 2000, I was invited to speak at an international seminar for city mayors "The New Millennium: Information Society and City Development" held in Guangzhou, China. I had visited China back in 1980, and when I arrived 20 years later, I could not recognize it. Advances in city transport and services were truly unprecedented. Watching the host, the mayor of Guangzhou, make his introductory remarks brimming with technical mastery of the subject, I felt embarrassed to follow with my modest keynote.

My speech focused on the vision of smart cities, and the challenges they raised for rapidly urbanizing China. I did not elaborate on ICT solutions in front of such a technology-savvy audience. I contrasted the old vision of a walled city in fear of invaders with a new vision of a smart city that is open and connected to ideas, trade, technology, and innovation. A key challenge for city leaders is to develop and communicate a vision for their cities that addresses the profound changes in their local, regional, and global environment, and that is inclusive of all stakeholders. Cities are hubs of innovation. They are the future. City leaders should understand the underlying mechanisms leading to innovation and competitiveness. They need to learn to anticipate, adapt, and drive change. They must collaborate across jurisdictions and mobilize all stakeholders: public sector, business, civil society, and academic institutions. These are not easy tasks.

I further described a world where mayors must manage public resources in light of declining central government support and rising local accountability. Rapid migration to cities represents an enormous challenge for most developing economies. It leads to the degradation of services and the environment and contributes to a vicious cycle of worsening income inequality. To counteract these tendencies, the service sector must become the largest employer and digital services must play a leading role in urban transformation. China is leveraging its traditional strengths in top-down city planning and intelligent infrastructure. But it should complement these strengths by harnessing public-private partnerships, citizen participation, and bottom-up innovation to shape the future of cities.

After my speech, I was surrounded by reporters asking difficult political questions about freedom of speech, openness to information, and data privacy. These issues were just emerging, even though cities have not yet become major collectors and users of data, and smartphones have not been invented! Even as I write this in 2023, smart cities raise profound issues and dilemmas about data privacy and security, state surveillance, and business surveillance. Smart cities based on extensive collection and use of data bring up new concerns about the government's unauthorized collection and use of personal data. Perhaps China is the most prominent illustration of this risk, but it is by no means alone.

Imagine a city where a driverless bus takes you to an unmanned supermarket or a hotel using a facial recognition system—a city whose residents and infrastructure are constantly monitored by artificial intelligence. This is not some dystopian vision of the future or a scene from a new sci-fi movie—it is reality in China.

Of about 1000 smart city projects in the world today, half are in China. Take, for example, the Xiongan New Area—a former backwater about 60 miles South of Beijing. Built entirely from scratch, it embodies China's future city vision and can become a model for the world to follow.

Some experts do raise concerns about what really is driving China's smart city boom and what it implies for residents, given that the smart city initiatives involve collecting large amounts of personal data. The Chinese government argues it is driven by pragmatic considerations: the need to increase the efficiency and effectiveness of China's rapidly growing cities, improve transportation, communication, environmental management, and crime prevention. China is experiencing rapid large-scale urbanization that requires modern, data-driven, intelligent social governance. The commitment to smart cities was firmly established by the Chinese government in its 12th Five-Year Plan in 2011. In the years since, Shanghai, Beijing, Guangzhou, Xi'an, Yinchuan, and Hangzhou have become notable examples of older urban areas that have received smart city makeovers.

In Hangzhou, a city in East China with a population of 10 million, City Brain, an AI smart city system designed by tech giant Alibaba, has been used for traffic management since 2016. By monitoring every vehicle in the city, City Brain has helped reduce traffic jams by 15%. Its creators claim it can optimize traffic for the entire city, predict where traffic jams will occur, and even prevent traffic accidents by instituting preemptive traffic control and policing.

India's Smart City Program

Digital India includes an ambitious smart city initiative that will gradually cover 100 cities. It aims to mobilize multiple sources of finance. Given the poor state of traditional infrastructure in Indian cities, the initiative has focused on improving its efficiency and on e-government, but will increasingly include data-driven smart city solutions. It is an example of a large but relatively poor country with ambitious plans to catch up and transform its cities to effectively meet service demands and sustainability challenges.

India's Smart Cities Mission (SCM) was launched by the Government of India (GoI) to develop 100 Indian cities as engines of sustainable economic growth and to improve the quality of life for citizens. The objective of the mission was to develop replicable models of inclusive and sustainable development for Indian cities by providing financial assistance to 100 cities selected through a competitive process. The Ministry of Housing and Urban Affairs (MoHUA) was responsible for the implementation of the Smart Cities Mission over a five-year period (2015–2016 to 2019–2020) with a significant budget outlay, complemented by funding from foreign governments (Japan, Singapore, UK), foreign private businesses and multilaterals. Each selected Smart City has set up a Special Purpose Vehicle (SPV) to implement the mission.

Urban growth in India is predominantly unplanned and unstructured and this has a negative effect on land productivity and creates energy-intensive patterns of growth. A big challenge in pursuing smart city solutions to urban development is to make a quick and sharp shift from an agriculture-based economy toward a manufacturing and services economy that can provide sustainable livelihoods for the Indian population. In India about 52% of total population, 632 million Indians are below the age of 25, and another 21% are between the ages of 15 to 25 (in 2022). Smart cities offer them an opportunity to improve their quality of life based on access and equity. Most Indian cities are deficient in basic services, financially weak and lacking the capacity required to plan and implement change. Without a radical change, Indian cities will continue to achieve limited growth at the cost of high and unsustainable resource consumption. The ambition and scale of the urban transformation in India will only be sustainable if the path chosen is a 'green' one. Better planning, technology, and management should become the cornerstones of India's urban strategy.

India has therefore adopted a three-level strategy for managing the process of urbanization. At the first level, poverty alleviation, affordable housing, and cleanliness are the three biggest challenges. National programs for Urban Livelihood, Urban Housing, and Urban Cleanliness are under implementation in all the 4300 cities and hence impact the entire urban population. At the second level, basic urban infrastructure development is the focus in 500 cities that have populations of over 100,000 people. Finally, at the third level, 100 cities are being developed under the Smart Cities Mission (SCM) to support "ease of living" by evolving a new paradigm of urban governance with citizens at the core and harnessing appropriate digital technologies to improve urban infrastructure, services, and optimal resources utilization. These 100 smart cities are more like a pilot project that will later be scaled to all the 4,300 cities across the country.

The Government of India acknowledges the need for reliable urban data. Sharing urban data on a common e-platform is essential to identifying green growth potential and envisioning smart interventions. This challenge is increasingly addressed by growing digital connectivity, big and open data platforms, and complementary national programs such as digital government (NeGP), and unique identification (UID or digital ID) program. For the Smart Cities Mission's digital strategy, a stack-based approach has been developed with the three pillars—People, Process, and Platform, driven by national-level technical standards and guided by a set of overarching design principles.

With a renewed focus on the digital economy and greater ambition being directed at the urban sector in India, there is a unique opportunity for articulating and adopting green growth strategies that can profoundly change the somewhat bleak prospects of Indian cities and trigger new enthusiasm for sustainable trajectories for achieving prosperity. Technology-enabled leapfrogging is also possible. But there are risks if the smart city program is misdirected toward "technology for its own sake," rather than aimed at achieving SDG goals of urban economic development, livelihood creation, development of urban physical infrastructure, and green growth into joint or complementary programs. If ICT and urban development are integrated successfully, India may provide a model of how "smart city" can be a game-changer for other (low and middle income) developing countries.

Reflecting on the Indian case, I identified several issues and challenges.

First, in a large and diverse country with many emerging and large cities, Bank assistance had to focus at the national and/or state levels, with an eye on shared platforms and solutions replicability. On the digital front, the ICT team was working at the state level to promote the development of smart cities across the state, for example, develop shared cloud-based platforms to support hundreds of municipalities in each state.

Second, there is a clear tension between focusing smart city initiatives on city-level digital technology platforms, on the one hand, and traditional infrastructure development and management—on the other hand. At times this tension leads to cooperation (cross-support or co-TTLs) within a lending operation, and at others, to competition for resources, and/or separate parallel operations. Some TTLs have navigated and balanced these tensions across GPs, but existing incentives do not support such behavior, and cross-support alone does not substitute for managerial coordination at the Bank—among GPs, and within cities—among sectors and departments. The Bank needs a clearly defined approach for these multi-sectoral expertise projects where specialists from different GPs work on their independent components, but the components are then woven together through a common program-based approach.

Third, there is a legitimate concern that the smart city brand is gaining the attention of national and city leaders and of the powerful national ICT industry. And hence federal and state funding may be diverted at the expense of depleted traditional urban infrastructures and management systems. The Bank needs to work on a strategic approach (like India's 3-level strategy) where current critical infrastructure needs are aligned with the future smart city vision.

Fourth, smart cities require existing digital infrastructure. For example, India's National e-Government Plan (NeGP) has built the necessary digital infrastructure (data centers, state-wide area networks, community service centers, national cloud, etc.) for each of India's 35 states and Union Territories. It also leverages 650 million mobile phone users enjoying a 90% decline in mobile internet costs. Bank teams need to build expertise to leverage a city's physical and digital infrastructures for efficiency and competitiveness.

Fifth, flexibility is needed in the Bank's approach. As of 2022, there is still no agreement on a proposed USD 480 million program to offer performance-based grants to select smart cities. Going forward, the Bank's new tech-enabled projects will inevitably become complex multi-sector data-driven programs demanding a much higher degree of management flexibility and creativity to address client needs.

Sixth, the scale of India's urbanization emphasizes the importance of getting its smart city program right. India's cities suffer from poor infrastructures, services, and governance. Significant ICT-enabled improvements via effective management and timely monitoring of finance, services, and infrastructures could go a long way toward alleviating poverty, conserving energy, and improving the local environment and climate.

Finally, India's experience may contribute to knowledge sharing among developing countries on ways to leverage smart city solutions in resource-scarce cities. Can technology help cities with weak municipal institutions and analog complements? What balance should be struck between traditional infrastructure investments and smart city solutions? Should major Indian cities be supported to create digital innovation hubs? Are Indian smart city solutions more frugal than those in developed countries?

Concluding

Digital technologies offer significant opportunities to transform urban infrastructures and services for sustainable development. The pioneering smart cities programs in India and China offer many lessons for urban development management at the national level. Smart cities like Singapore offers best practices as premier users of smart city solutions.

In this chapter, I explored some of the issues facing smart city planners: How can smart cities be designed and nurtured? How can smart city solutions contribute to inclusion rather than reinforce prevailing inequalities in access to public services? What are the merits of two competing approaches to smart cities, one emphasizing top-down solutions and open platforms, and the other calling for bottom-up innovation and the engagement of all stakeholders? Can these two approaches complement one another? What balance should be struck between investment in traditional urban infrastructures, on the one hand, and digital solutions—on the other hand? How should policymakers and aid agencies manage the dilemmas of data privacy and security, "state surveillance" and "business surveillance" arising from the extensive collection and use of data in smart cities?

Smart Cities development assistance should be guided by the fundamentals of smart city transformation: shared vision, clear strategy, realistic targets; local leadership, institutions, and governance; human capital, technological and data capabilities; collaboration and partnerships; adequate finance; and local capacity for localization and innovation.

The integration of digital technologies into cities is likely to cause many unpredictable effects, such as changes in urban density, spread of urban settlements, enhanced highway safety via connected cars and traffic control, better accountability of city governments, more or less inclusion, and higher risks of cyberattacks on city infrastructures. Getting smart city done right is critical to the majority of the urbanized world, and the resilience and future of the planet. The integration of the emerging smart city digital ecosystem with traditional urban infrastructures calls for building local capacity to experiment, adapt, and innovate to manage this integration.

CHAPTER 7

Learning from Pioneering Country Experiences

Abstract This chapter compares the ways countries adapt national digital transformation strategies to advance economic development goals. While national ambitions and goals for pursuing digital transformation may vary, key foundations and dynamics are shared. They present a rich learning agenda. Lessons of experience are distilled from pioneering countries for policymakers and business leaders, and for educators and researchers to develop diagnostic tools and conceptual frameworks to advance the nascent discipline of digital transformation. Singapore strategy has evolved over time, and recently included an artificial intelligence strategy.

Keywords Singapore strategy · Comparing countries · Emerging lessons · Learning agenda

Two studies were important in World Bank learning and my advocacy journey: *The Diffusion of Information Technology: Experience of Industrial Countries and Lessons for Developing Countries (1995)*; and *the East Asian Miracle and Information Technology: Strategic Management of Technological Learning (1996)*.[1] Both studies were carried out at a time when many World Bank economists believed that common government failures

[1] Hanna et al. (1995, 1996).

N. K. Hanna, *Driving Digital Transformation in Developing Nations*,
https://doi.org/10.1007/978-3-031-54573-3_7

in promoting technology and industrialization justify keeping governments out of developing national policies and strategies for technological transformation. A proactive role for government would automatically amount to industrial policy, protectionism, picking winners, and wasting resources.

At that time, the Bank sponsored a major study on the East Asia Miracle (World Bank 1993). The report tried to square the circle—rapid growth with equity, without conforming to the Washington Consensus. It identified the policy and institutional innovations that led to superior economic performance, yet suggested that this success was not replicable in other developing countries outside of East Asia. The studies I co-authored suggested otherwise: both OECD and East Asian countries pursued more coherent national policies and strategies to harness the ICT revolution for their competitiveness and accelerated development.

The diffusion study drew on the evaluation methodology and analytical framework that my collaborators have developed and used to assess the effectiveness of OECD's technology diffusion programs in participating countries. We covered the diffusion programs of eight OECD countries, and interviewed various stakeholders including universities, research and technology transfer institutions, management consulting firms, trade associations, and beneficiaries (small and medium enterprises, SMEs) to capture their diverse and complementary perspectives. The study examined the determinants of effective diffusion and analyzed national IT portfolios to draw lessons and trends. We discovered that since the late 1980s, industrial countries have shifted their emphasis away from supporting national champions toward diffusion and aiding SMEs in the adoption of available technology. There was a clear recognition that adoption has its challenges and requires several phases of learning and capacity building. The study drew guidelines for designing these programs for maximum impact: programs should be packaged to provide integrated services to differentiated users; technology and user sophistication should guide the choice of delivery institutions: universities, private consultants, trade associations, public industrial extension, etc.

The diffusion study suggested broad directions for adapting these lessons to the developing countries environment. National strategies must address incentives, institutions, and capabilities for adoption. Various instruments should be explored to improve access to international best practices that are beyond the search capabilities of most SMEs. It is important to promote institutional learning capabilities and engage business leadership and private sector associations. Concerned government agencies should learn to partner with the private sector and become catalysts for diffusion. Experimentation, monitoring, formal and information evaluation, and continuous adaptation are critical. Low-cost diffusion programs are possible. They should rely on local institutions and associations to speed up learning and knowledge transfer. To maximize benefits, complementary investments in intangibles must accompany ICT investments. The VP for private sector development signed off on the study. The challenge was to create the staff capacity to absorb and practice these lessons.

The East Asian study focused on technology "catch up" and competitive advantage "creation." It aimed to shed light on the ignored part of the East Asian miracle story: the extraordinarily rapid rise of the IT industry and its role in producing higher value goods and services. While not attributing this "miracle" to a single factor, the study tried to redress the balance by focusing on the role of strategic policies affecting technological learning and sustained productivity improvements. Hence, East Asia's (Korea, Singapore, and Taiwan, China in particular) success can be largely attributed to its anticipation and follow-through of the new opportunities arising from the ICT revolution and the provision of consistent support to industries that leveraged technology to help their economies transition from labor-intensive to knowledge-intensive production. They set ambitious performance goals, stretched their comparative advantage, and made commitments to a particular set of skills well ahead of the market. Their shared view of the future guided investments in core competencies, management of public-private coalitions, search for strategic alliances, learning, and experimentation. They also developed policy, planning, and management processes that were agile, collaborative, and learning-oriented.

The New Industrializing Countries (NICs) of Asia recognized ICT as a strategic industry, a general-purpose technology, and an essential infrastructure. They also leveraged ICT to improve traditional infrastructures like transportation, pioneer "intelligent" infrastructure, electronic trade networks, public information utilities, etc. Intent on diffusing ICT and building national information infrastructures, the NICs devised novel programs, set up technology diffusion groups, and incentivized ICT multinationals to test advanced ICT applications. Public-private coalitions and partnerships helped focus national resources, speed up learning processes, demonstrate the advantages of ICT applications, build information networks, and exploit complementarities and externalities. National ICT strategies evolved through the use of agile planning. Societal learning was at the heart of these processes.

These studies demonstrated that economy-wide digital transformation requires considerable policy and long-term institutional innovation, experimentation, and learning and that consensus-oriented strategic management can be learned. Digital transformation also demands local knowledge sharing, capability development, partnerships and participation of private sector and local government. It is a process of strategic collaboration between the public and private sector, to identify constraints and opportunities for digital transformation. It calls for measures to capture global opportunities and address country-specific conditions, institutional constraints, and market failures and strategic opportunities.

Pioneering Strategy of Singapore[2]

The Singapore case illustrates the broad spectrum of national digital strategies. Its early steps are very relevant to transitioning and follower countries while its more recent experience is a global best practice. Singapore has been among the first to pursue a comprehensive and continuously adaptive strategy for digital transformation.[3]

In 1990, I invited the CEO of the largest software company who was also a key contributor to the country's national IT plan to speak to the then skeptical Bank management about the Singaporean experience. Since then I had the opportunity to visit Singapore, to meet PM Lee Kuan Yew, and to study the country's transformation journey and its strategic public-private partnership.

Singapore is a compact, highly urbanized island city-state that has benefitted from the continuity in political leadership and an early decision to push for digital technologies-driven transformation to a knowledge

[2] For more in-depth description of Singapore and the other 7 country cases, see Hanna and Knight (2011a, b). I also draw on D. Lin (Dec. 2016, LinkedIn) of McKinsey & Company.

[3] I chose Singapore for this book because of its systematic digital transformation over time with visible results. But examples of India and Sri Lanka, and my research across countries confirm the many ways and paths countries can take to digital transformation as a function of their political economy, initial economic conditions, etc. Context matters!

economy. Successive 5-year ICT Master Plans guided by a long-term vision were implemented since 1980. Singapore now boasts a highly advanced e-government and digital economy legislation system that contribute to its competitiveness. Leadership ambition, commitment and foresight, intelligent broadband infrastructure, widespread Internet access and digital literacy, targeted sector digitization programs, and an attractive business environment have brought Singapore to the frontiers of the digital economy. The aim continues to be to generate digital capabilities and innovation that contribute to solving big national challenges.

Singapore's digital government evolved in line with each National ICT plan to bring about changes to the way the Singapore government works, interacts, and serves the public. An outcome-focused stakeholder-centric Singapore e-Government Framework is used to monitor the maturity of digital government through key performance indicators. This approach has been applied systematically to three major groups of stakeholders: employees, businesses and customers, and citizens—using a "whole of government" approach to achieve process efficiencies and integration across different agencies. For example, common databases accessible to many agencies and e-services were established for people, organizations, vehicles, and land.

Singapore implemented a shared government-wide digital infrastructure and a suite of services. Digital competency was pursued through increasingly sophisticated training for the general public. Digital specialists and champions were identified to lead digital government implementation. Supporting programs were nurtured in schools, institutions of higher education, and professional associations. Change management programs and a conducive policy environment were developed to facilitate changes in business processes and build confidence in electronic transactions.

Collaboration between the government and private sector has been intense. In the early years, the state retained its traditional role of owner and operator of key ICT assets and infrastructure, but encouraged active private sector participation in government projects through tenders, calls for collaboration, competitive dialogues, and technology trials. Investment by international and local companies was strongly encouraged. As an innovative and competent pool of ICT companies grew, government gradually shifted from planner, implementer, and owner of ICT and its assets, to that of master planner and facilitator, encouraging greater competition. It thus provided a supportive environment in which ICT companies were able to thrive, grow and diffuse their products. Through innovative partnerships with the private sector, the government is now able to foster a digital economy, protect against technology obsolescence, and create further employment in the development and delivery of ICT products. In doing so, the government is further catalyzing the growth of the ICT industry.

What makes Singapore a digital leader, and what does it plan to improve? First of all, the guiding plans for Singapore's digital transformation, including the *Infocomm Media 2025*, set ambitious goals, such as becoming the number one in the world in using digital technology to create economic and social value. Public and business leaders are challenged to devote considerable effort, creativity, and resources to achieving them. Secondly, government leaders, starting from the Prime Minister, have been strong proponents of Singapore's digital government and digital literacy efforts. At times, such enthusiasm has led to overlapping responsibilities among several public entities, including the Government Technology Agency, and the Smart Nation Program (housed in the PM office).

Many groups have a say in the government's digital strategy. The Committee on the Future Economy aligns the digital government strategy with the long-term national economic strategy. It enables government leaders to fit the digital government strategy to the needs of citizens and businesses. Digital efforts in the public sector push businesses to digitize faster than they might have otherwise.

Recruiting and developing talent is a priority for government and business. In government, the Center of Excellence was established to provide technology services to other government agencies. The government is investing in citizens' digital skills, and the Skills Future program is helping workers keep their capabilities current. Retaining talent in the country by providing incentives for training in local and multinational enterprises located in Singapore, and attractive career paths in public services for young Singaporeans are also key.

Singapore's experience in nurturing digital entrepreneurs offers many lessons. As of 2017, SMEs make up over 99% of Singaporean enterprises and contribute nearly half of Singapore's gross domestic product. The delivery model of Singapore's startup promotion and innovation agencies is heavily centralized within its economic agencies under the Ministry of Trade and Industry. It is premised on strong inter-agency coordination between two key implementing agencies: the Economic Development

Board (EDB) and Enterprise Singapore (ESG). ESG assists SMEs at various stages of their growth through a comprehensive suite of assistance programs. ESG manages the Local Enterprise Association Development (LEAD) program which partners with industry associations to fund broad initiatives to improve the capabilities of their members. LEAD is complemented by the Capability Development Program (CDP), which directly assists SMEs to improve capabilities at the enterprise or strategic grouping level.

A critical element contributing to the success of Singapore's approach is the strength of coordination between government agencies. In addition, support programs are systematically aligned with the firm's stage of development, ensuring that the SME has a broad menu of policy instruments tailored to its needs to support and finance upgrading. Support begins with ESG direct assistance and gradually involves other economic agencies to help increase the firms' capabilities, matchmake with multinational corporations (MNCs) or large local organizations (LOs) and to identify new markets for expansion or R&D.

Such programs are not without challenges. Singapore's entrepreneurship and innovation programs have adopted a strong top-down approach. While this has the advantage of ensuring coordination across government agencies, it limits the involvement of business chambers and trade associations in the design and implementation of these initiatives.

Singapore continues to strive to create an attractive ecosystem for the digital economy. It leverages its size and location to bring global players in the digital industry such as Google and IBM to co-locate, partner, and collaborate. It offers its city as a gateway to Asia, and a test-bed for new technologies, by providing advanced communication infrastructure and innovation environment. Global players have set up their regional headquarters and innovation centers in Singapore. For example, Singapore provided an attractive location for IBM's Blockchain Innovation Center focused on security issues in logistics and fintech as home to the world's largest port and the third largest financial center.

Singapore's progress was reflected in various international digital economy rankings where it continuously scored near or at the top. In 2016, for example, Singapore was first in the World Economic Forum's Networked Readiness Index that measured ICT-driven economic competitiveness. In some areas, however, such as ICT usage by individuals and businesses Singapore was ranked lower, so the government set out to help individuals and companies to adopt and benefit from digitalization through the Skills for Digital Workplace initiative and the SME Go Digital program. Public leaders also recognized the need to do more to make digital Singapore more inclusive, including soliciting the inputs of underserved groups, such as older Singaporeans and SMEs. They also planned to cultivate more creativity in the excellence-driven education system. To keep pace with technological advances and sustain its leadership position, Singapore leaves no room for complacency.

Singapore's journey in digital transformation is an inspiration for late adopters. In the early days of its independence, Singapore faced daunting challenges: ties with Malaysia were cut, unemployment and crime were high, urban slums proliferated, half of the population was illiterate, racial and religious tensions were on the rise. With limited land, Singapore struggled with land use planning, transportation, and industrial cluster development.

Openness to the rest of the world was not a choice but a necessity dictated by its near total lack of natural resources. Country leaders abide by the belief that Singapore's continued survival depends on its ability to play a useful and valuable role in the world. This has inspired Singapore's development and underpinned its governance foundations: openness, connectivity, links with the rest of the word, and global relevance through innovation.

National Artificial Intelligence Strategy

Leveraging its achievements in building a digital transformation ecosystem, Singapore began to design and implement a national AI strategy. It published its AI strategy in 2019: *advancing smart nation journey*. The strategy is composed of two broad programs: building the national AI ecosystem, and embarking on national AI projects. Critical ecosystem enablers are:

- partnership between the research community, IT industry, and government—to enable rapid commercialization and deployment of AI solutions;
- AI talent and education—to address shortfall in skills across the entire range of AI-related jobs;
- data architecture—trusted data sharing framework to enable quick and secure access to high-quality cross-sectoral datasets;

- trusted environment—to build trust in AI technologies to enable test-bedding and deployment of AI solutions;
- international collaboration—to shape the international AI discourse.

An initial tranche of national AI projects has been identified to deliver strong social and/or economic impact for the nation. These projects are expected to guide investment in AI research, prime demand to anchor local talent and capabilities, demonstrate value of AI and collaboration, and guide how the country builds up its supporting digital infrastructure.

Singapore's AI approach emphasizes rapid deployment, learning, and capability development. It focuses on key sectors of the economy with high impact, and for which they can build on existing strengths and comparative advantage. For Singapore, these sectors are: transport and logistics, finance, manufacturing, smart cities, health care, education, government services. Projects also include the enabling digital environment: cybersecurity and safety and security. The strategy aims to tighten the AI deployment loop: fast learning from implementation.

Comparing Country Cases

Later studies I conducted in collaboration with Peter Knight and others on digital transformation, covering eight countries, further confirmed Rodrik's dictum: *One Economy, Many Recipes*. No "one size fits all" strategy (Rodrik 2007; Hanna and Knight 2011a, b). In-depth country experiences are indispensable to learning new practices, capturing tacit knowledge, and building frameworks and theories. Case studies of country experiences convey a more realistic picture of the messy creative processes involved—they offer researchers material for theory building and hypothesis testing, while practitioners can learn from best practices. They help engage scholars and practitioners in dialogue on strategies for building a knowledge society. They also demonstrate the role of frameworks and conceptual models in guiding strategy design and implementation and the need to improve these models further.

Country or economy-wide cases enable researchers to capture important interdependencies among key elements of a country's digital transformation ecosystem. At the Bank, I chose to work first as a country officer as I was convinced that the country is a better "accounting unit" for learning and evaluation than separate projects.

National digital transformation strategies and programs are typically communicated in planning documents. Similarly, aid agencies present ICT programs and projects for financing in final blueprint not process terms. That gives the impression of a highly controlled, deductive, linear planning exercise, starting from a comprehensive analysis and ending with a comprehensive blueprint, or starting from an isolated pilot that is fully designed and appraised upfront.[4] The reality is quite different. *Like all strategies, those related to digital transformation seldom emerge fully developed.*

Using a case study to examine the process of digital transformation strategy formulation and implementation can make important contributions to our understanding and practice. First of all, it offers a model for practitioners to reflect upon their own practices, become participant-observers, and help contribute to multidisciplinary research on national ICT strategies. Secondly, it captures the political and institutional dynamics that shape digital development strategies. Early political backing and coalition formation, timely mobilization of resources, dynamic negotiation of priorities, and sequencing of implementation are often neglected in the reductionist recasting of ICT deployment for development. Yet, these are critical aspects of strategy design, implementation, and sustainability. Finally, a case study of the strategy development process allows for contextual understanding of the linkages and interdependencies among the various elements of digital transformation.

Unlike common descriptions of national ICT strategies, the country cases I discuss reach beyond a static assessment of the knowledge economy and e-readiness to capture the dynamics of developing and implementing a strategy and of building e-transformation partnerships within a country. They leave behind the typically long laundry list of recommendations for transforming a country into a digital or knowledge economy and reflect the hard choices and tradeoffs that must be made in designing and implementing digital development within real-life human, financial, and institutional constraints. They take account of initial conditions, stakeholder interests, institutional learning, and political dynamics.

The literature on country experience in developing and implementing digital transformation is growing. But, with few exceptions, that literature

[4] For discussion of the project cycle and its limits for non-engineering projects, see Hanna and Picciotto (2002).

is either theoretical or descriptive. Descriptive literature typically depends on official statements of national ICT policies and strategies, with scant attention to implementation experience, evaluation, and lessons learned.[5] Even scarcer is the literature on comparative experience in pursuing digital development and transformation.[6]

I believe case studies are of interest not only to ICT and technology policy experts but reach a broader audience to support inclusive transformation, including development practitioners, policymakers, and national and international development consultants and researchers.

In my work, I developed several criteria for cross-country process comparisons. These "process" criteria are of fundamental importance to country digital strategy design and implementation. They include integration of digital transformation in a country's development strategy; comprehensiveness, synergy, and coherence of the ICT strategy; e-leadership, stakeholder engagement, and institutional mechanisms for implementation. They also capture the balance between top-down management and bottom-up initiative, between pursuing long-term and short-term objectives, and between ICT as a cross-sector enabler and an industry on its own. The final set of criteria for comparing e-strategies includes reliance on innovation and adaptation during implementation; attention to monitoring, evaluation and measuring outcomes; addressing the digital divide and social inclusion.

Emerging Lessons

Evaluating and sharing country case studies is critical to advancing the field of digital assistance. Development practitioners often focus on the easily standardized and measurable indicators: investment in ICT hardware and software, telecom penetration, Internet connectivity, etc. This gives an incomplete picture of digital development and is not conducive to holistic thinking and learning about the intangibles that are harder to

[5] Individual country case studies have been covered in successive issues of the annual Global Information Technology Report, published by INSEAD and the World Economic Forum (WEF).

[6] A notable exception is "National E-Strategies: A Review of 40 Countries" Chapter 5 in World Bank, 2006.

measure, but no less important. These intangible assets are the accumulation of knowledge in people, institutions, and processes. They come from systematic learning-by-doing and evaluation.

In reviewing country cases, it was hard to find reliable information on the quality of implementation or independent results evaluation. Almost all reviews of national ICT strategies are self-reporting exercises, even when issued by international organizations (ITU 2010), and many mainstream economists remain skeptical about the self-reported cases of the transformative impact of ICT. Objective evaluation and systematic learning about digital development are difficult to come by. Using holistic and systematic assessment toolkits for the digital economy combined with independent evaluation can help.

To advance development thinking and practice, systematic learning and evaluation must be taken seriously. Country capacity for monitoring, evaluation, and learning in this emerging field should be built from the ground up. It must be holistic and participatory. Holistic digital economy assessment tools should be developed further. Evaluation and learning will require policies and incentives to mobilize demand for good governance and social accountability, including accountability for online services and open data—through enhanced citizen access to information about service delivery and digital dividends. Communities of practice within and across nations should be encouraged to share experience and support along the journey of digital transformation.

Most countries are still at the early stages of their digital transformation journeys and have much to learn from themselves, each other and from the pioneers. There is no substitute for the process of experimentation and self-discovery. Developed countries have created several regional forums (including the EU, the WEF, and the OECD) to share knowledge and provide support to policymakers.

Developing countries have the opportunity to learn from the experience of frontrunner countries while inventing their own best practices for a perfect fit. Newcomers to high-income country status like Korea and Singapore have leapfrogged, learned fast, became test beds for innovation, and started to partner with the most advanced countries. Learning from these good practices should help countries and local governments build capacity to master the digital transformation process.

Developing countries may establish their own communities of practice at the regional and global levels. New development partners like India, China, Korea, Singapore, Brazil, and South Africa are creating their own South-South partnerships. Global development agencies can provide knowledge platforms and nurture communities of practice that cut across all levels of development. The Bank can offer a learning platform using its Digital Development Partnership (DDP), a multi-donor trust fund established in the wake of the 2016 World Development Report.

A Learning Agenda for Researchers and Policymakers

Some emerging lessons can be drawn from the experience of the leading countries. These are best framed here in terms of a learning agenda for researchers and policymakers of transforming countries:

- How can a country pursue a holistic and long-term transformation strategy? What can be done to sustain commitment and reconcile the pressures for quick wins with the longer-term investments in institutions and foundational projects?
- How should the institutions of digital transformation be designed to provide maximum support for national development goals and harness the global digital revolution for local dividends?
- What measures can help align and integrate the national digital transformation strategy with the development strategy? How can local content and application development be supported to advance development priorities?
- How can leaders strengthen the synergies within the digital transformation ecosystem?
- What lessons from industrial policymaking of the past can be applied to digital transformation policymaking?
- What complementary factors will be needed, economy-wide and in each sector, to realize the digital payoffs? What roles should policies, institutions, and leaders play? How can policymakers address the often-neglected, softer aspects of transformation, such as managing change, skills, incentives, and culture?
- How should policymakers engage stakeholders, build coalitions, and pursue partnerships to create and implement a shared vision? What roles can the local ICT industry and civil society organizations play?

- What measures are necessary to secure digital diffusion and inclusion? How early should affordable access and universal digital literacy be pursued to realize equitable and sustainable transformation?
- What balance should be struck between strategic direction and local initiative? Can both be aligned to create a virtuous cycle of innovation and societal learning?
- How can policymakers support experimentation, innovation, and adaptation? How can they enable fast learning, agile monitoring, and participatory evaluation?

CHAPTER 8

Mastering Transformation and Digital Dividends

Abstract A key message of research, including the World Bank's, is that maximizing digital dividends and closing the digital divide require a better understanding of how technology interacts with other elements of development—that is the "analog complements." Countries need to strengthen regulations that allow firms to connect and compete; develop skills that technology augments rather than replaces; and build institutions that are capable and accountable. The author draws on this research and his own to underline the key challenges to realizing the digital dividends, and the growing transformational possibilities for developing economies. He then draws lessons on mastering digital transformation as a learning process and as a vibrant innovation ecosystem.

Keywords Research · Digital dividends · Analog complements · Transformational possibilities · Mastering transformation process

Since my retirement from the Bank, I have gradually moved beyond digital access and applications toward conceptualizing digital development as an interactive process and a transformative ecosystem. In this chapter, I first reflect upon the Bank's 2016 Digital Dividends World Development Report (World Bank, WDR 2016) which attempted to untangle the many factors that affect digital investments dividends and assess the operational

N. K. Hanna, *Driving Digital Transformation in Developing Nations*,
https://doi.org/10.1007/978-3-031-54573-3_8

impact of this report on the Bank's development assistance practice. I then summarize my view of digital transformation as a social learning process and a dynamic ecosystem as I examine the challenges and opportunities inherent in this transformation. I refer to Singapore's digital transformation journey as a case study and conclude with key recommendations and lessons learned for countries aspiring to master the digital transformation process.

Researching the Digital Dividends

I was pleasantly surprised when the Bank announced digital technology as the theme for the WDR 2016. I have actually suggested this theme for one of the annual WDRs years back in a staff manifesto of 1991. The response took 25 years! It was also a surprise given the Bank research department's consistent reluctance to address future-oriented issues of technology and innovation. I also wished this research were shared with Bank economists who were often skeptical of the role of technology policy in accelerating economic development and hostile to my suggestions to address client needs through lending and technical assistance operations.

What were the Report's takeaways on digital dividends? Digital technologies can be transformational by promoting inclusion, efficiency, and innovation. They can significantly reduce the costs of economic and social transactions: the costs of acquiring information, making decisions, and monitoring and enforcing transactions. The Report claimed that despite many success stories, the aggregate impact of digital technologies has been less than expected. Benefits have not been fully realized.

Certain benefits have been offset by new risks. In the absence of accountable institutions, public sector investments in digital these technologies amplify the voices of the elites. Benefits are not widely shared. Concerns about job losses, cybersecurity, misinformation, content restrictions, etc. increase. There are no simple answers, but the questions deserve vigorous national and global debate. The digital divide is still wide, both in access and capability. About four billion people have no internet access. Digital divides persist across income, age, geography, and gender. Even when internet access is available, affordability remains a major challenge and access costs still vary greatly. Among those connected, digital capabilities also vary a lot.

A key message of the WDR 2016 is that maximizing digital dividends and closing the digital divide require a better understanding of how technology interacts with other elements of development—what the Report calls "analog complements." Countries need to strengthen regulations that allow firms to connect and compete; develop skills that technology augments rather than replaces; and build institutions that are capable and accountable. To benefit the most, countries need to create a proper technology environment. Digital development strategies must be much broader than just ICT strategies.

What was the impact of the WDR Report? I agreed with its key messages but questioned its operational impact on the Bank and client countries (Hanna 2016b). In my view, the Report was too cautious about the potential of the digital revolution, perhaps to avoid a clash with the predominantly conservative economists-dominated culture at the Bank. I had several stimulating conversations with Deepak Mishra, lead author of the Report, a young and bright development economist. He had enough challenges and did not feel responsible for operationalizing the Report's findings.

I requested a meeting with the WBG's Chief Economist to convince him to proactively facilitate the operationalization of the Report, but he was not interested. Budgetary and turf issues have limited the participation of the Digital Development Department (DDD) in both the drafting and the dissemination of the Report, yet the operationalization of this major research document seemed to be left to the DDD. Yet, while attention was focused on sharing the Report's key messages with the development community, DDD's budget and staffing for operational work were cut. Incentives continued to maintain the massive gap between research and operations. The WBG's Board failed to notice this contradiction.

Fortunately, a Digital Development Partnership (DDP) trust fund was subsequently created to help further operationalize Report findings. The DDP fund offered a platform for digital innovation and development financing. The DDP brought public and private sector partners together to catalyze support to developing countries in the articulation and implementation of digital development strategies and plans. For example, the DDP made it possible to develop a methodology for assessing the digital economy and pilot it in many countries, mainly in Africa.

Challenges to Digital Transformation

How can development practitioners help harness digital technologies to deliver significant digital dividends to developing countries? How can policymakers harness the digital revolution for accelerated development?

Digital technologies hold the promise of being a game changer for global development. But the much-anticipated impact of this technological revolution is still a potential. Digital dividends including inclusive and sustainable economic development, improved governance, and responsive public service delivery have been limited thus far. They do not add up to transformative development outcomes. Diffusion, scaling, and effective innovation is what can cause significant socio-economic impact.

Three key challenges bedevil the design and implementation of digital transformation programs that aim to realize the developmental impact of digital technologies.

First, digital technologies, infrastructures, platforms, and applications are highly interdependent and should be treated holistically as a dynamic ecosystem. This ecosystem includes information and communication infrastructure, digital platforms for identification and payments, a local ICT services and digital entrepreneurship sector, technical ICT skills and leadership, and content and media industries. It also includes digital applications for government and business, enabling cyber policies, and ICT-sector management and regulatory institutions. Maximizing digital dividends requires assessing and nurturing this digital ecosystem and tapping into its synergies at the national, local, and sector levels.

Second, capabilities to plan and implement national digital strategies are increasingly important to engender a shared vision and mobilize a long-term commitment to digital transformation. ICT opportunities and investments must be integrated into national and sectoral development strategies to promote investment in broadband infrastructure and shared digital platforms, to adopt complementary policies, and to establish the required institutions. Stakeholder engagement and partnerships with civil society and the private sector are a must to ensure wide diffusion and inclusion, and enable local initiative, adaptation, and learning.

A digital transformation strategy should be developed in continuous interaction with the national development strategy and as a crosscutting enabler of priority economic sectors. Attention to building local policy and planning capabilities is much needed to provide strategic direction, to plan and implement digital projects, and to adapt planning processes to diverse local contexts.

Third, digital transformation demands substantial investment in organizational capabilities, process innovation, institutional learning, and other intangible digital assets (such as digital content). Little attention is usually given to these technological and institutional learning capabilities in developing countries, where these capabilities are needed most. Yet, best practice suggests that investments in ICT-related process improvements, training, and reorganization should exceed investment in ICT by a ratio of 4 or 5 to 1. Profound changes in skills, roles, norms, routines, teamwork, cross-sector partnerships, and leadership and managerial practices are necessary, especially in developing countries where complementary assets and coordination mechanisms are missing, responsibilities for policies and leadership are fragmented across government, the digital transformation ecosystem is weak, and ICT specialists are often separated from development specialists in education, governance, and other sectors.

I proposed an integrative framework to guide the thinking about the digital transformation ecosystem in order to pursue coherent policies and reinforce ICT-enabled development initiatives (Hanna 2016). The framework can help policymakers and stakeholders identify interdependencies, missing links, and binding constraints in the ecosystem. It calls on policymakers and regulators to break out of the ICT bubble and engage with the developmental context to be transformed.

Transformational Possibilities

Transformation possibilities are growing fast, and so is my proposed learning agenda.

First of all, what are the strategic approaches to transforming government? How can a whole-of-government approach be adopted? How can policymakers and development practitioners mobilize and respond to demand for better services, promote public-private partnerships, and monitor the performance of service providers? What are the best platforms and practices that can be leveraged for public sector transformation?

Secondly, how can sector-wide transformation be applied to education, health, financial services, and agriculture, and other sectors?

Thirdly, what steps can be taken to promote digital communities and an inclusive information society? How about establishing funds for grassroots innovation and community-driven local content development, for example?

Finally, how can business leaders and policymakers promote digital transformation in business? How can digital technologies be used to reduce government transaction costs and improve the business environment? What policies and platforms should be adopted to facilitate e-commerce and open trade? One example is the promotion of e-commerce which depends on multiple policies and capabilities at the enterprise, network, and national levels (Hanna 2016a).

Mastering the Transformation Process

Mastering the digital transformation process demands upgraded managerial and technical skills, digital leadership institutions and networks, enabling policies and regulations for a digital economy, a high-quality communication infrastructure, and a competitive local ICT industry able to learn from local and global practice.

Strategies to strengthen educational institutions and prepare them for the digital age are needed. Policymakers must define clear roles for the government, the private sector, and development partners, and to build institutions able to orchestrate and implement various elements of the transformation process including developing broadband strategies to promote supply, mobilize demand, secure universal access, support the ICT services industry in diverse contexts, and develop a vibrant digital transformation ecosystem.

CHAPTER 9

Diagnosing and Managing Digital Ecosystems

Abstract This chapter shares the evaluation of a new digital assessment methodology to assess the readiness of countries, and potential strengths and pitfalls of using such assessment tools. Digital transformation assessment holds the potential of mobilizing the necessary country-level leadership and digital leadership institutions. Diagnosing a country's digital transformation ecosystem calls for substantial collaboration between sectoral development practices within aid agencies and within countries. Another challenge is the multiplicity of complements (policies, skills, institutions) needed to realize the promised benefits. This calls for a more comprehensive conceptualization of the digital transformation ecosystem and coordination throughout implementation. A key challenge is to link digital assessments to the ultimate development goals of eliminating absolute poverty and secure shared prosperity.

Keywords Country digital assessment · Digital diagnosis · Digital assessment methodologies · Link assessment to poverty · Collaboration

N. K. Hanna, *Driving Digital Transformation in Developing Nations*,
https://doi.org/10.1007/978-3-031-54573-3_9

In 2019–2020, at the request of the Bank, I carried out a just-in-time evaluation of a pilot assessment program, including assessment frameworks, tools, and processes deployed in select pilot countries.[1] My report was based on interviews with many of the staff who carried out country assessments and generously shared their impressions.[2] I enjoyed these interviews as they allowed me to capture rich first-hand experiences that are seldom shared or candidly discussed within the Bank. I am grateful to all the colleagues I interviewed as they complemented my own impressions of country assessments during my brief direct engagements in the early stages of the process. Unfortunately, the Bank seldom provides open and candid forums for sharing client engagement experiences and thus misses a key opportunity for organizational learning.

Aims and Methods

The digital development department (DDD) was in search of a methodology to assess the digital economy of its client countries, potentially in collaboration with other key global practices. The aim was to create a digital economy toolkit to help client countries understand their current level of digital adoption and potentially engage with them in the development of future digital transformation strategies. The Russian Federation pioneered the development and execution of such a holistic digital economy assessment. While the Russian government was working on the development of a comprehensive digital economy strategy, a Russian think tank led by Yuri Hohlov was interested in partnering with the Bank to develop a digital economy assessment methodology. I had the opportunity to take part in this effort together with Rossotto and his team.

The emerging methodology drew on many existing international indicators of digital development as well as on in-depth interviews with key local stakeholders and members of the digital transformation ecosystem. In its final form, DECA (the Digital Economy Country Assessment) was strong in its links to a sophisticated client, its depth of engagement with

[1] My review was funded by the Digital Development Partnership, a multi-donor trust fund to finance innovative approaches and projects in digital development.

[2] "Assessing the Digital Economy" *Journal of Innovation and Entrepreneurship* 9:16. https://doi.org/10.1186/s13731-020-00129-1.

stakeholders on the ground, and its breadth of sectoral applications analysis. Its limitations included complexity—covering over 200 indicators, reliance on country-wide averages even in large countries like Russia, and an emphasis on an advanced ICT sector—raising concerns about DECA's replicability in other countries.

In the meantime, the DDD, the Finance, Competition and Innovation department (FCI), and the IFC were busy developing another assessment methodology called Digital Economy for Africa or for All (DE4A) focusing on diagnosing the five pillars of the digital economy: digital infrastructure, digital platforms, digital financial services, digital entrepreneurship, and digital skills. DE4A enjoyed wider global Bank practices ownership, deeper DDD management commitment, and localization for African countries. When done collaboratively, these country diagnostic reports helped to bring together teams from otherwise competing Bank organizational units.

For a while there, each methodology had its own supporters, with the DECA model used in the East European and Central Asia (ECA) Region, while the DE4A was applied to Africa. Other WBG Regions were not committed to either approach at that early stage and were hoping to match the scope and depth of their assessments to their regional needs, opportunities, and levels of development.

I tried to reconcile the competing assessment methodologies and reduce the turf battles by opening up a forum for discussing the advantages and limitations of each methodology. Both DECA and DE4A were evolving—it was difficult to hit moving targets! Reconciling the two methods proved difficult, mainly due to differing assessment philosophies. This, together with my candid criticism of the limited environment for experimentation and learning ultimately led to DDD management's embargo on my final report. To be fair, I think some progress in addressing these issues has been made since my review. Hopefully my candid evaluation provided just-in-time feedback at an early stage of institutional learning to enable systematic digital diagnosis.

Since 2020, the DDD worked with other departments and the IFC to build a digital development toolkit covering different foundations and aspects of the digital economy. The Digital Development Toolkits aim to help identify challenges and necessary policy and regulatory actions in digital development; analyze potential solutions; and provide practical examples from countries that have addressed digital development-related matters. Their target audience includes policymakers, regulators, researchers, and other relevant stakeholders in the digital development field, particularly those in developing countries. The series of toolkits consists of the Broadband Strategies Toolkit (https://ddtoolkits.worldbankgroup.org/broadband-strategies), the Cross-Sector Infrastructure Sharing Toolkit (https://ddtoolkits.worldbankgroup.org/infra-sharing), the Cloud Readiness Assessment Toolkit (https://ddtoolkits.worldbankgroup.org/cloud-readiness), the Engendering ICT Toolkit (https://ddtoolkits.worldbankgroup.org/gender-toolkit), and the Digital Capability Framework (C:\Users\nagyhanna\Desktop\Digital CapabilityFramework).[3]

This expanding toolkit funded by DDP, the recently-established multi-donor trust fund, represents a recent but substantial investment in analytical tools to enable the diagnosis of the digital economy in developing countries. These kinds of toolkits did not exist during my early attempts (2000–2018) to diagnose levels of digital adoption and develop digital economy strategies. It may be too early to assess the impact of these diagnostic tools on the quality of dialogue with country counterparts, capacity building, and digital transformation strategy development. In the short term, the toolkits can help standardize the Bank's diagnostic reports. In the longer term, they should be leveraged to build local capacity and provide a holistic view of the digital ecosystem, as well as to help prioritize policy reforms and investment.

Common Challenges in Country Assessment

My evaluation report focused mainly on diagnosing a country's overall level of digital economy development. It identified common challenges and lessons learned from applying these assessments in different country contexts. These challenges include addressing inequality and poverty issues, securing participation and partnership of stakeholders, clarifying and prioritizing digital adoption goals, addressing institutional and implementation challenges, and integrating digital transformation strategies into country development strategies. Other challenges include stimulating digital innovation and entrepreneurship, mobilizing local demand for new

[3] https://www.worldbank.org/en/topic/digitaldevelopment/brief/digital-development-toolkits.

technologies, engaging business in digital diagnostics, adopting multidisciplinary and whole-of-society approaches, and collaboration across sectors and practices.

Inclusion and poverty have been left out of the digital economy assessment toolkits. The reasons for that are twofold. One is the lack of participation of relevant global practices in the preparation and implementation of digital diagnostics methodology. Limited participation of the Social, Urban, Rural, and Resilience Global Practices resulted in failing to account for major spatial inequalities. This was important for a large, diverse country like the Russian Federation on India, where national averages for digital economy indicators miss local variation. Other missing Global Practices were the Poverty and Education; Health, Nutrition, and Population; and Governance global practices. Participation of the regional chief economist's office would have been important for inclusion and the broader development agenda.

The second reason is insufficient disaggregated data such as internet usage by income groups. The International Telecommunications Union (ITU), for example, generates data on the number of households with internet access but not necessarily on internet usage or how this varies across income groups or across regions. Given its expertise in development data, this is a gap the WBG could help fill.

To illustrate this point further, none of the sample pilot countries made reducing inequality and alleviating poverty a central focus of their digital diagnosis and strategies. Yet, unless harnessed for inclusive development, digital technologies are likely to contribute to rising inequality. Evidence shows that the aggregate impact of digital technologies is highly uneven among and within developing countries. At the same time, many of these technologies, such as, for example, mobile money, offer new and significant opportunities to reduce poverty and achieve shared prosperity.

The assessment tools I reviewed did not provide adequate coverage of digital inclusion and income inequality at the national and subnational levels. Current national-level assessment indicators were too aggregate to capture digital-related income, gender, and geographic disparities. Assessments often failed to explain the persistence of barriers to inclusion: what explains slow and uneven adoption? How effective is Internet access in contributing to poverty reduction? Why do promising applications for poverty reduction fail to scale? What mechanisms are needed to counter the monopolistic tendencies of digital platforms and digital industries?

Assessments did not attempt to systematically track the distributional and empowerment impact of the new technologies.

Concern about poverty and inclusion has implications for both: what is being assessed, and the way the assessments are carried out. Assessment tools should be accessible to all stakeholders so that the diagnosis is not limited to a dialogue with the elites. Pilot country assessments did not devote much attention to empowering representatives of poor communities and social intermediaries to participate beyond the supply of data. Assessment results were not used to engage poor communities in shaping and implementing an inclusive transformation strategy.

Implications for Countries and Aid

The experiences drawn from the digital economy assessment program helped me draw several broad lessons for both developing countries and aid agencies (Hanna 2020). First of all, it is crucial to develop digital *leadership* in countries and aid agencies. Effective leaders communicate their vision of how the digital economy contributes to inclusive growth and poverty reduction. They allocate the necessary budgetary resources for staffing, training, partnerships, and organizational learning and ensure that digital economy strategies are integrated into country development strategies. It is important to seek and nurture such leaders and change agents. Second, it is important to build the necessary *skills* within the country and aid agency to help clients harness the digital revolution. Local capacity to implement is often taken for granted. Third, to develop and disseminate the emerging digital assessment *tools* while attending to the *process* of using and implementing them effectively. Fourth, to address *poverty and inequality* challenges as integral parts of assessments. Finally, to create a country- and agency-wide knowledge sharing and *learning* platforms.

Key elements of the digital transformation ecosystem reside in different parts of the aid agency and in the country. A holistic approach to digital economy would demand *ecosystem-wide leadership and coordination* (Hanna 2007b; Hanna and Qiang 2009). The failure to implement this approach has created a major challenge to collaboration and integration in the pilot countries under the current WBG's operating model. A common practice in WBG lending operations was to focus on investments in information infrastructure and digital applications without a critical examination of the institutional setting and leadership commitment which ultimately determine the outcomes of these investments. The holistic approach to diagnosing the digital economy may provide an opportunity for country and aid leadership to bring coherence to digital transformation initiatives and encourage collaboration and learning.

It is important that investments in digital foundations and sectoral applications are mutually supportive and synched with the broader development agenda. Ministries in charge of establishing the digital foundations should aim to support key sectors such as education, health, finance, trade, and agriculture. Sectoral transformations usually require policy and institutional investments that build on the digital foundations.

Digital economy assessment holds the potential of mobilizing the necessary country-level leadership and digital leadership institutions. Assessments should include institutional and stakeholder analyses to engage public agencies and business and civil society organizations in the co-leadership of the digital economy. Assessments should aim to induce country-based coordination and policy coherence among major aid agencies and sources of finance for the digital economy.

It is also important to focus on the process, participation, and partnerships involved in digital assessments. The process used to assess the digital economy critically influences outcomes and impact. Yet, little thought is usually given to the process, particularly to the quality of interactions between the assessment team and country stakeholders. The process may be driven by various objectives such as promoting client participation and ownership, forming coalitions and partnerships, developing capacity and institutions, mobilizing local knowledge, or simply writing a fact-based diagnostic report. The diagnostic process can also vary in response to urgency, client capability for follow up, and/or available windows of opportunity, such as a newly-elected, reform-minded government.

The process that was followed in the pilots I evaluated varied. Usually, a lot of attention was given to the tools, data collection, and reporting—often at the expense of engendering successful ownership of the results and their effective use. The degree of local stakeholder participation in the digital assessment and downstream strategy development varied greatly. Little effort was made to influence the composition of the local participating team to include intermediary institutions representing small business, civil society, trade and professional associations, and poor communities. Pilots could have benefitted from upfront stakeholder analysis to guide participation and collaboration within the country.

Local anchor institutions were critical to securing a responsive, client-driven assessment process. The degree of securing effective and inclusive participation was influenced by the designation of a capable anchor institution and its own capacity to engage key stakeholders. Few pilots sought to secure broad and balanced participation. Fewer yet were involved in mobilizing underrepresented groups and engaging social intermediaries.

Engaging business as an equal partner in shaping a country's digital strategy remains a key challenge for developing countries and aid agencies. While significant progress has been made to secure collaboration between the Bank and its private sector arm, much remains to be done to engage IFC in the full cycle of assessment, strategy formulation and implementation, and downstream investments. Full IFC engagement in the digital economy would require that WBG prioritize upstream policy reforms that unlock opportunities for the deployment of private sector solutions in the digital economy. It would also call for the prioritization of investments in local digital businesses that can contribute to the digital economy ecosystem. It would necessitate aligning staff incentives to reward collaboration among WBG institutions in digital economy assessments and strategy implementation. In other words, a cultural shift from tactical to strategic partnership between the World Bank and the IFC is a must.

Similar challenges have arisen in securing collaboration between government agencies, the digital sector, and the user businesses in the pilot countries. In my review, effective engagement of the private sector in the digital assessment was constrained by the presence of local monopolies, weak representation of small businesses, mistrust in the government, and a limited understanding of the assessment methodology.

Another challenge of conducting digital assessments has to do to with *learning and knowledge sharing*. Digital transformation demands accelerated social and institutional learning. Assistance to countries to pursue digital transformation demands agile, intensive, and collaborative learning. The Bank's pilot-based approach to these assessments works well to stimulate learning, but organizational learning was constraint by the pressure to lend money, publish results, and adapt tools to contexts. It is also important to ensure that pilots are managed and evaluated differently from traditional technical assistance or lending operations.

Assessment tools, processes, and reports should be shared widely among aid agencies and countries. The lack of a standard assessment methodology should leave space for debate, learning, and creativity. Local universities and think-tanks must be encouraged to pilot and institutionalize assessment tools, while international organizations should collaborate to improve their effectiveness and to coordinate donor activities.

Digital assessment practice depends on a culture of collaboration, risk-taking, learning from mistakes, openness, and trust. Assessments should be viewed as opportunities for dialogue and learning with stakeholders. The creation of shared platforms would leverage the considerable economies of scale involved in collecting data and applying analytics.

Digital assessments leading to elegant reports should not be an end in themselves. They must engage government and business leaders in strategizing for holistic digital transformation. They must help build partnerships across different economic sectors in a country, within the WBG, and between development partners.

One overarching lesson is the importance of adapting the diagnostic and assessment tools to country context and giving attention to building coalitions and facilitating policy reforms, periodization, and implementation processes. This requires bridging the common gap between ownership at the top government level or the ministry of ICT, and other stakeholders (inside and outside government and the lower ranks of civil servants) involved in implementation. The *process* of constructing or adapting diagnostic tools is critical to broad understanding and acceptance of the results of diagnosis and the subsequent design and implementation of digital transformation strategies. The process of identifying stakeholders (beyond a single champion) calls for stakeholder analysis upfront and designing a process to engage them and build ownership over time. Many digital assessments have been carried out by outsiders, mainly by short-term international consultants and researchers. They often produced lengthy documents without commitment to implementation and without clarity about the "how" to translate good intentions into good practice to drive digital transformation.

Independent Evaluation Response

My key findings and recommendations were subsequently incorporated by the Independent Evaluation Group (IEG) in its 2021 *Mobilizing Technology for Development* report. Perhaps my most important finding was the disconnect between the execution of digital assessments and the twin goals of ending extreme poverty and boosting shared prosperity. The IEG evaluation further confirmed most of my findings regarding WBG preparedness, including the level of organizational ability and organizational willingness to collaborate in this area—as reflected in staff skills and mindsets, internal processes and procedures, and institutional culture and incentives. It concluded that, despite some areas of strength, "the WBG is *not yet sufficiently well prepared* to help clients harness the opportunities and mitigate the risks posed by disruptive and transformative technologies" (DTT). Hopefully, this was a wakeup call for the WBG.

Digital technology practice needs to be distinguished from other emerging technologies for several reasons. First of all, as a general-purpose technology, it affects all economic sectors, hence we speak of the digital *economy* and the digital transformation of all industries and services. So far, no other set of technologies has come close in ubiquity. Other DTTs are typically confined to one sector and should thus be addressed by the sectoral staff—without much need for cross-sectoral coordination over shared infrastructures, platforms, and ecosystems.

Diagnosing a country's digital transformation ecosystem calls for substantial collaboration between sectoral development practices within aid agencies and within countries. Another challenge of digital transformation is the multiplicity of complements (policies, skills, institutions) needed to realize the promised benefits. This calls for a more comprehensive conceptualization of the digital transformation ecosystem and coordination throughout implementation. The digital technology revolution causes an explosion of data and the growth of AI, IoT, and other new fields. These fields demand even broader diagnosis, risk management, and cybersecurity than other disruptive technologies, calling for prioritized and targeted changes in international development practices.

CHAPTER 10

Conclusions: A Country Learning Journey

Abstract How should digital development strategies be pursued at the economy, government, and city levels? This chapter offers suggestions for country policymakers and aid professionals on ways to accelerate digital transformation. Lessons of experience are organized into five fundamental challenges: enabling holistic and sustained transformational change; empowerment and ownership; leadership, institutions, and human resources; experimenting, learning and evaluating; and inclusion and diffusion. They apply equally to practitioners, countries, and aid agencies.

Keywords Country learning · Holistic transformation · Empowerment · Ownership · Leadership · Institutions · Experimenting · Inclusion

The digital technology revolution and the accompanying data revolution create new exciting avenues for development and offer a sense of hope about solving its long-standing challenges. They also raise new public policy challenges and risks, ranging from the future of work, global monopolies, and rising inequality, to surveillance, security, privacy, misinformation, digital fragility, and algorithmic biases. These opportunities

N. K. Hanna, *Driving Digital Transformation in Developing Nations*,
https://doi.org/10.1007/978-3-031-54573-3_10

and risks are too critical to the future of development to be left to technology specialists or government bureaucrats alone. It is a long learning journey for all involved: a marathon, not a sprint.

My experience highlights five fundamental lessons or practices:

- Enabling holistic and sustained transformation;
- Engendering empowerment and ownership;
- Building leadership, institutions, and human resources;
- Experimenting, learning and evaluating; and
- Prioritizing inclusion and diffusion.

These fundamentals are equally relevant to practitioners like you and me, as well as to countries and aid agencies. I offer few suggestions for policymakers and development practitioners to navigate their learning journey. A check list of emerging best practices is also attached as (**Annex 1: Best Practices**).[1]

Enabling Holistic and Sustained Transformation

The first overarching lesson is the need for policymakers and digital development practitioners to shift their attention away from an excessive focus on global rankings, single technologies, and standard strategies. They should promote holistic approaches, continuous learning, institutional reform, and change management processes to fit the local context. Digital economy strategies should focus less on single technologies in favor of broader strategies to digitalize priority sectors—adopting an ecosystem approach to enable the transformation of an entire sector or economy.

As conceptualized earlier and in Fig. 1.1, a digital transformation ecosystem approach would cover digital communication and data infrastructure, public and business digital platforms, digital financial services, digital innovation ecosystem, and digital skills and literacy. It would also include digital policies and institutions to promote trust and security in data transactions. Developing a dynamic, inclusive, and safe digital economy would require nurturing the interaction among these

[1] I developed this summary list of best practice as I co-authored the 2030 CAREC strategy (Asian Development Bank 2022). The list should be adapted over time to reflect recent local and global experience and new emerging lessons.

components in order to bring about a vibrant and coherent digital transformation ecosystem.

Among these key ecosystem components, I would single out human resources development: digital literacy to ensure effective adoption and inclusion, specialized digital skills to establish and manage the digital infrastructure, and digital leadership to lead the transformation process at the national, sectoral, and institutional levels. This ecosystem foundation is a long-term determinant of success of digital transformation. It requires wide-ranging educational reforms. This challenge is often taken for granted by the technical (ICT) ministry and aid donors. Often, it is left for the ministry of education to grapple with alone. That leaves a major gap in the ecosystem. My experience in many countries shows it is essential for the education ministry to collaborate with other ministries, universities, private training institutions, business associations, and NGOs to train talent for the digital economy and maximize the dividends of a national digital transformation ecosystem.

Why is it taking us so long to adopt an ecosystem view of digital transformation? Is it mainly due to the sectoral and organizational silos within governments and aid agencies? Does the prevailing quantitative approach favor fewer variables and correlations, irrespective of complements and contexts? Does the short-term perspective of aid agencies and consulting firms favor standard blueprints and segmented approaches to holistic transformation?

Taking a holistic approach is likely to increase the complexity of projects than focusing on one element of digital transformation and leaving it to local government or aid recipient to deal with coordination and integration among various elements of the ecosystem. Or perhaps ignore the complementarities and interdependencies among these elements.

The challenges of adopting a holistic approach should not discourage the Bank or national governments, as it is essential for sustained transformation. It is key to tapping synergistic and scale effects that drive the digital sector. The potential payoffs of digital transformation for the economy are substantial and do increase dramatically with time. A narrow approach that focuses on connectivity, or the ICT industry alone, delays and reduces potential benefits. A holistic approach to digital transformation is a paradigm shift in development thinking and practice that is worth the effort. A creative part of a digital transformation strategy is to focus on the most binding constraints and critical complements, to prioritize, phase and sequence, and to help build local capacity to manage complexity over time.

Digital technologies can play very different roles depending on the needs of specific countries. These roles require *foresight capability and strategic thinking* about national and global development in the digital age. The national election cycle is too short to capture long-term possibilities, analyze potential consequences, and think through future scenarios. Building a strong foresight capability and future orientation are essential for holistic and sustained digital transformation. Such transformation often requires trading short-term pain for long-term gain. Sustaining popular support requires demonstrable outcomes in the short term. A key path to true transformation is to balance a portfolio of quick wins (to capture low-hanging fruits and garner broad support) with long-gestating investments (to create local capabilities and complementary institutions). This challenge is particularly felt in countries with fragile economies and democracies, as in the case of South Africa and Brazil.[2] Making the necessary tradeoffs would facilitate social consensus and cohesion.

Successful countries take advantage of new waves of technologies, but do not rush into investments without experimentation, governance, capacity building, and continuous evaluation and learning. They recognize that digital transformation is not about chasing the "next big thing" or investing in the latest technology as an end in itself. They persistently build e-leadership institutions and agile governance mechanisms to mobilize change agents and technology adopters. They induce changes in the culture to support collaboration across the digital ecosystem and encourage a tolerance of risks associated with innovation. They experiment with the latest technologies without losing sight of the fundamentals and the intangibles.

Although digital technology can accelerate development, economy-wide digital transformation is still a long-term process, and its dividends may take decades to arrive. Political pressures to produce quick wins and tangible results in the short term are real, and must be addressed, however, the expectation that each ICT application is transformational and the "irrational exuberance" generated by digital industry innovations

[2] This tension between short- and long-term objectives and mechanisms to manage this tension are illustrated in detail in the case study of e-Sri Lanka (Chapter 5).

often lead to "hype cycles" and "bubbles."[3] Development practitioners and aid agencies are also prone to succumb to development "fads" in search of silver bullets and rapid solutions to long-standing and pressing development problems. Unless pilots and quick wins are complemented by institutional and policy reform, investment in fundamentals and shared platforms, they will likely be short-lived and not worth the effort.

Successful countries strike an appropriate balance between long-term vision and near-term action. A long-term perspective secures continuity and guides near-term polices and investments. It facilitates the adoption of a holistic and coherent approach to national digital transformation strategies. A comprehensive view of digital technologies for development requires the prioritization, selection, sequencing, and phasing of the most critical investments in view of the overarching objectives, and the availability of resources and capabilities. A long-term perspective would anticipate and manage systemic interdependencies and the foundations of the digital economy. Without taking account of key synergies and interactions in a timely manner, true transformation is unlikely to occur, to be sustainable, or to be diffused on a large scale.

Digital transformation programs should be phased and aligned with local capacity to manage complexity. Adopting an ecosystem approach does not mean acting on all the elements of the ecosystem at the same time. It means focusing on the foundations of the ecosystem at an early stage and on the critical missing elements that may affect the country's digital transformation success in the long term. It also means identifying changes that are actionable in the short term and can provide demonstrable dividends and build political support to continue longer term policy and institutional reforms. Often this would mean prioritizing those digital transformation applications that are easier to implement in specific priority sectors. The interplay between those foundations and the applications should guide the sequencing and coordination in a country's digital transformation strategy.

The deeper digital transformation and more intensive institutional reforms take time to experiment, implement, and mature. Financing

[3] Like the Dot.com bubble of 2000, and perhaps the emerging social media (e.g., Facebook) bubble.

instruments and technical assistance practices should be tailored to these long-term requirements.[4]

Phasing and sequencing digital transformation can help focus on key objectives, and on mutually reinforcing interventions to achieve them. For example, Singapore adopted a holistic and ambitious vision of digital development from the start, but it pursued this vision over successive and sequenced e-strategies. It started with a focus on foundational and mutually reinforcing projects for digital infrastructure and platforms, e-literacy, and digital government, with a few quick wins, then became increasingly more inclusive through phasing and upgrading (Hanna and Knight 2011b).

These broad lessons need to be applied at the country level based on its SWOT (Strengths, Weaknesses, Opportunities and Threats) diagnostic. A one-size-fits-all strategy can indicate weak country ownership of such a strategy. Country specificity is key. A cookie-cutter approach to digital strategies should be avoided perhaps by doing through SWOT analysis. Such analysis should be open and transparent. It should engage multiple stakeholders. Superficial SWOT exercises often miss leveraging the specific strengths and opportunities while ignoring the weaknesses and the risks. Each country has different possibilities and paths for progress in digital transformation. Prioritizing and sequencing will vary depending on initial conditions and the comparative advantage of a country.

Of course, not every country can emulate India's evolution with substantial investment in digital skills to become a major exporter of software and IT-enabled services. India underinvested in broad and basic education, and this led to less inclusive dividends from the local digital industry. Few can follow this example. Instead, the biggest developmental payoff is likely to come from applying and diffusing digital technologies in the domestic industries and services. Countries should not equate digital transformation with an advanced digital sector. They can still aspire for comprehensive digital transformation with appropriate local skills and IT industry capabilities that are strategically focused on adapting and applying digital technologies to domestic industries and institutions.

[4] Development Policy Finance (DPF), a financing instrument of the Bank, may be a promising vahicle in focusing on ecosystem-wide strategies, policies, and institutions.

Engendering Empowerment and Ownership

Empowerment and ownership call for identification of the country's stakeholders and understanding of the political economy. Who should be empowered? How can we operationalize and measure such vague but critical concepts as ownership and empowerment? How can we avoid "the tyranny of experts"?[5]

Practicing empowerment and engendering ownership of stakeholders require changing the incentives and practices of aid professionals. Both tacit knowledge and analytical tools are needed to master the art of empowering clients to identify existing problems and develop digital solutions. Policies, strategies, and assessment tools should aim to expand choices for local stakeholders, and the poor in particular.

Having "the client country in the driver's seat" is easier said than done (Hanna and Picciotto 2002). Who is the client? Would client "compliance" with aid agency conditions mean ownership? Should ownership be extended beyond the core technology or digital economy ministry? How can the ICT ministry engender ownership and empower user ministries to pursue best practices in digital transformation? Would public-private partnerships be needed to bridge the digital divide and promote inclusive transformation?

It is important to encourage local stakeholders to develop a shared vision of digital transformation objectives and of the means to achieve these objectives. This shared vision should explain the relevance of digital transformation to economic development, and to the welfare of various stakeholders. Creating such a vision involves coalition formation and capacity building to move from e-vision to strategy, planning, and program implementation.

An integrated ecosystem approach to digital development also requires broad ownership and coordination capabilities across stakeholder institutions. It calls for an upfront effort to build local capacity and nurture partnerships. For example, the e-Sri Lanka case demonstrates the importance of ecosystem ownership at the national level—through the creation of a national ICT Agency at the highest levels of government. The e-Society Innovation Fund, a component of e-Sri Lanka, helped create "home-grown" digital solutions by and for poor communities.

[5] Easterly (2015).

Despite the challenges to engendering local ownership and empowerment, such country-centered engagements were the most rewarding to me and my country counterparts. I was the recipient to many warm farewells, recognitions, and friendships in the countries I served. Just to quote one, on my departing from the e-Sri Lanka project, I was honored by Lalith Weeratunge, Secretary to the President of Sri Lanka with this quotable statement: "Let me, as I have done on many earlier occasions, thank you with much admiration and appreciation. You have been the best external friend Sri Lanka has had for many years. Your sincere advice, guidance and above all being tough with us when its necessary to do so, have been the best contributory factor towards all our victories in the realm of ICT."

A sense of urgency is often needed to build sustained commitment to digital transformation. Countries that accelerate their development through digital transformation are often driven by an economic crisis or a sense of vulnerability which they turn into an opportunity for transformative change. Transformative leaders create and communicate this sense of urgency to broaden ownership and mobilize stakeholders to act. It is difficult to accept and sustain transformation in complacent bureaucracies. My study of early transformers and fast followers shows how this sense of urgency, combined with a vision for change, was widely shared in countries like Singapore. Some other early adopters like Finland and Estonia faced economic shock that brought about a strong national consensus on the need to digitally transform their economies. On the other hand, technologically advanced countries like Brazil who did not share a common vision and a sense of urgency for digital transformation fell behind in their transformational journeys and global rankings (Hanna and Knight 2011a, b).

In the cases of India and Sri Lanka, ownership inside and outside the government had to be built over time, with outsiders limited to a potential catalyzing role: building on the initial support of the relatively few local reformers and seeking to nurture and empower those reformers. Strategies to build ownership had to be tailored to core ecosystem components and targeted to key stakeholders and levels of government. The case of India suggests ownership can start with the ICT industry and young educated entrepreneurs linked to global demand for ICT skills, who in turn can advocate public policy and ecosystem-wide reforms.

Building such ownership was at the heart of designing and implementing India's digital development strategy. Much of engendering ownership was carried out by political leaders and the technocrats at the Ministry of Electronics and Information Technology of India. They had to learn to play this new leadership role. But equally important was the role of the software and IT services industry. The Indian information technology sector lobbied the government for opening the telecommunications industry to competition, and for liberalizing foreign trade for computers and services. The tech sector provided much of the local technical capabilities needed to adopt ICT in government and the local industries. This paved the way for Aadhaar[6] (unique identification system) and other public-private partnerships for public services. The IT sector of Sri Lanka, although less mature than India's, also played an important role in shaping the e-Sri Lanka program. Owning a shared vision of the future of IT, the tech industry continues to play a critical role in leading the digital transformation of the economies of the Asian Tigers and China.

Closely related to ownership is the issue of mobilizing local demand and forming coalitions for digital transformation. Digital transformation in the government and enterprise sectors of the developing world is less constrained on the supply side than on the demand side. Digital innovation is undercut by the lack of demand from its potential users in public and private agencies. The supply side of the digital ecosystem (such as access to internet services and digital platforms) is better understood and managed by technology suppliers and producers. The demand side is less understood and measured, thus neglected or taken for granted. This contributes to underinvesting in leadership, institutions, skills, and content most needed by potential user organizations, particularly by lagging public institutions and small businesses. Developing countries also miss the benefits arising from demanding users and user-producer interaction.

Policies and programs to stimulate demand for and diffusion of digital adoption may include competition policies, cyber security, digital culture and literacy, locally-relevant content development, and demand for open data and good government (Hanna 2018). High impact applications (killer apps) like digitizing land ownership records in India led to more adoption and demand for other on-line services. Social intermediaries also

[6] Aadhaar ecosystem comprises of core digital infrastructures with the objective of providing enrolment, update, and authentication services for all kinds of online public services.

play important roles in building informational capabilities among rural communities and poor neighborhoods.

Digital culture and literacy are key to inclusive and sustained transformation. Cultivating digital culture may include adopting digital-first delivery of public services, citizen-centric services, use of analytics for decision-making, and collaboration and cocreation with citizens. It demands creating a trusting digital environment that promote the collection and use of data taking account of privacy and ethical guidelines. It requires cybersecurity awareness and training. Mass media and communication campaigns proved to be helpful in spreading digital awareness and culture in cases of rural communities I worked on in India and Sri Lanka.

Country ownership of digital transformation is critical to mobilizing local learning and implementation capabilities and to accelerate mutual learning with outsiders. Local understanding and ownership of the digital diagnostic tools and processes are preconditions for successful and sustained implementation. They require a thorough understanding of the political economy, who can lead and champion digital transformation, and who benefits and who loses from various transformations of the economy. The processes of diagnosing the digital economy and of designing transformational strategies and programs can critically shape local demand and ownership. These processes should build local alliances and partnerships for change. They should aim at deepening and broadening ownership over time. Digital transformation implies deep rooted change and that takes time.

Ownership is often viewed through the perspective of the donor agency, with failure to reform by the client country attributed to weak country ownership. Yet, anyone who wants to help—outside the country or inside—should start by understanding the way major national stakeholders perceive existing challenges and opportunities. Outside agencies must understand that they can only help those countries that want to help themselves while nevertheless playing a catalyzing and influencing role. Ownership is not a given. Often, it needs to be nurtured and sustained, yet in my experience, the Bank tends to take ownership for granted.

What should be the role of outside helpers? Aid agency staff and international consultants tend to exaggerate the importance of their role. Yet, outsiders can only hope for a catalytic role in digital transformation. They are tempted to impose or sell their own diagnostic tools, bureaucratic processes, and standard short-term solutions. They often ignore country specificity in terms of preconditions for transformation. Yet, the

India, Sri Lanka, and Singapore cases point to the crucial role of having local coalition among powerful actors in government, business, and civil society to drive digital reforms. Outsiders may have global knowledge and cross-country experience, but they are constrained by their own agency's priorities and the short-term horizon of their engagements. Academics are limited by their focus on research methodologies, which are not typically used for engendering local ownership and action learning. Outsiders can only be partners in short part of a long-term locally-driven journey. Their success is in offering timely small steps to the right set of stakeholders and facilitates the formation of local coalitions and institutions for change and learning.

How to help people help themselves? Autonomy-compatible assistance requires outside helpers (development practitioners) to start where the doers (country stakeholders) are. Helpers have to see through the doers' eyes. Doers would remain in the driver's seat. This principle comes from a range of fields—psychology, pedagogy, and management (Ellerman, in Hanna and Picciotto 2002). My own best experiences followed this principle. This mode of development assistance secures local ownership, avoids cognitive dependency, blends local and universal knowledge, tailors solutions to local implementation capacity, builds self-confidence and self-efficacy of the doers, and promotes local experimentation and social learning. It is the prerequisite for sustainable reform and transformation.

Building Leadership, Institutions, and Human Resources

Fast adopters of digital transformation attended first and foremost to the "soft infrastructure" of digital transformation: leadership, shared vision, enabling policies and institutions, upgraded digital capabilities, and national consensus and digital culture. They focused first on human resources, not just technology per se. They invested in human capital, and more specifically in training all citizens as information and internet users. Governments and businesses constantly sought to understand the needs of their clients and to engage them in the design and implementation of the transformation process. The further these countries traveled toward transformation, the broader and deeper these building blocks had to reach.

Strategy and policy matter, and so do leadership, institutions, and capabilities. The interplay between policies and institutions unfolds over time through a series of choices. Best designed policies and strategies do not implement themselves or get implemented by external actors. Political leadership, supported by a capable technocracy, is essential to formulating good policies and strategies, as well as implementing programs for positive outcomes. Local capabilities are essential for moving beyond idealized strategy design or a universally applicable policy template. One-size-fits-all-type policy or strategy does not work, particularly for an emerging field of development practice where much adaptation, experimentation, and tacit knowledge are needed for iterative design and implementation.

In most cases I studied, the state played active and expanding roles (Hanna 2018; Mazzucato 2013; Rodrik 2007). In the last decade, the scope of digital public goods, open data, and their regulation have increased enormously at the national and global levels. In collaboration with business and civil society, the state must play a critical role in managing the interdependencies and exploiting the potential synergies among various elements of the national digital ecosystem. The commitment of transformative political leaders is critical but their commitment should be institutionalized to ensure the sustainability of the transformation process.

Transforming countries build e-leadership institutions to promote, regulate, coordinate, monitor, and evaluate the digital development process. E-leadership institutions identify synergies across e-government, e-learning, e-business, and e-society.[7] Guided by a holistic framework of digital transformation, these institutions capture opportunities to tap potential synergies, realize returns to scale, and build cross-sectoral platforms. Digital government and digital citizen identification become open platforms for innovation and delivery of public and private services.

The process of identifying, organizing, and engaging key stakeholders in e-transformation is by no means simple or straightforward. It is a messy process. Who can speak on behalf of the various constituencies of the digital transformation ecosystem? Large and diverse countries as well as those involved in civil conflicts present special problems. Divides inherent in countries like South Africa, for example, can make the process difficult to manage. In these countries, there are no effective mechanisms for the government to engage with key stakeholders representing business, academia, and the civil society. Ethnic and racial

[7] The benefits of tapping these synergies have to outweigh the cost of coordination.

divides weaken engagement between the government and other stakeholders. Comprehensive institutional and political economy analysis is often required to understand the existing dynamics of communication, engagement or lack thereof, or the dominance of one stakeholder such as the telecommunications industry.

Transformative leaders seek to understand stakeholders and engage them as enablers, partners, and implementers. A digital strategy clarifies the roles and comparative advantages of all potential actors: government, private sector, civil society, and academia. Accordingly, it defines what roles each can best play in designing and implementing digital transformation programs. In doing so, it helps build partnerships and coordinate agendas. By building these partnerships, it creates an enabling policy environment for implementation and a healthy ecosystem for the digital economy.

New technologies open up new opportunities, but they also demand more transformative leaders, not less. Countries can "leapfrog" some technologies and adopt the latest advances, but they cannot leapfrog institutional and human resources development. Given the promise of the new technologies, countries are tempted to bypass the demanding development of the soft infrastructure.[8] But no off-the-shelf or "plug and play" technical solutions can substitute for institutional learning, change management skills, and in-house capacity to define institutional visions and user requirements. Taking full advantage of digital technologies and integrating and institutionalizing them on a large scale require new leadership competencies, including capacity to motivate knowledge workers, engage citizens, collaborate with partners, and manage "institutional openness" and social change.

Leadership and institutions for digital transformation can be developed at several levels. Leadership at the national digital ecosystem level is the most crucial and often demands the engagement of the President, Prime Minister, and/or Minister of economy and finance (Hanna and Qiang 2009; Hanna 2007b). In federated countries, good practices often arise

[8] The gap between the potential of ICT innovations and their widespread diffusion and economy-wide impact is significant, similar to earlier GPTs. The rapid diffusion of mobile phones may be the exception in view of the dramatic decline in costs and the low barriers and skill requirements for users. Yet, realizing the full potential of using mobiles for affordable internet access and for development-oriented applications may take more time.

at the provincial or city levels, as I witnessed first-hand in India and Brazil. Cities present dynamic digital ecosystems where synergies and innovation across sectors are more impactful and amenable to open leadership and cross-sectoral, smart solutions.

Digital leaders play multiple roles. They develop organizational capabilities to envision, manage, and scale successive waves of investments in digital technologies. They explain and communicate why digital transformation is necessary. They vividly communicate with key stakeholders the goals and raise the ambition for digital transformation for the country, sector, city, or region they lead. They articulate how to transform the vision into action and mobilize resources accordingly. They communicate the destination, sustain momentum, and support the transformation journey. They also accept the challenges and address the risks of transformation. They communicate to stakeholders the need for reskilling and for policy and role changes and resource allocation (Melhem and Jacobsen 2021).

In sum, digital leadership role is one of change management, which aims to build consensus, foster collaboration, mobilize change agents, and develop ownership for digital transformation of the country, government, city, or region. In my experience, it is rare to have one leader to excel in all these roles, and hence often is the need to build leadership teams across sectors and institutions. Special leadership development programs would be necessary, to model new behaviors, and lead people and institutions, not just manage technology.

Country leadership at the digital ecosystem level is essential. It can be nurtured and facilitated through external assistance, combined with local change agents. Countries face learning barriers similar to those at aid agencies that are often amplified by government silos and the lack of digital leadership skills and incentives. Pioneering countries focus on developing and communicating a shared vision and building local capabilities, partnerships, and coordination mechanisms to overcome inertia and capture ecosystem-level interdependencies. Aid practitioners can play a valuable role in nurturing collaboration and co-ownership of digital transformation strategies across government departments together with business and civil society stakeholders.

National digital strategies are often designed by international consultants or main staff of the digital ministry. They tend to focus on large investments and complex projects that can be centrally funded and managed to achieve economies of scale. But these centrally-driven programs often lack mechanisms to promote bottom-up initiatives, build capacity at the grassroots, and induce innovative partnerships between central and local organizations—all critical to mobilizing local knowledge and innovation capabilities and achieving scalability and sustainability.

Effective country adopters of e-transformation build dynamic networks of leaders and leadership institutions across sectors, spanning government, business, civil society, and academia. Transforming countries progressively broaden their leadership institutions and networks. One major payoff of digital economy strategies and plans is the consultation process and the diverse institutions, networks, and coalitions that are built during the planning process.

Effective adopters of e-transformation are also effective implementers. They do not stop at developing politically-appealing visions of the digital economy. The vast gap in transformational outcomes between Singapore and South Africa was primarily due to the latter failing to address institutional and implementation weaknesses, change management, and human resources development. While leadership at the top is always crucial, advanced adopters build a robust institutional infrastructure within and outside government to sustain and deepen digital transformation.

The distinguishing features of effective implementation by successful adopters are the strength of e-leadership institutions, a focus on developing and nurturing champions and chief-information officers (CIO), and training a meritocratic civil service. Other critical success factors are: bringing various players in the industry to partner and innovate in government-funded pilots, and agility and adaptation during implementation.

Developing e-leaders or CIOs requires more than strengthening technical expertise. In many countries CIOs have been selected for their technical expertise and up-to-date knowledge of the latest digital technologies. In some countries, CIOs are chosen for their business and budgetary skills, perhaps at the level of deputy minister, covering a variety of functions. Others come from people management functions. Rarely are they a hybrid of the above, or experienced in change management. Indian educational institutions and academies, among others, have developed specialized courses for CIOs and digital leadership more generally. These programs can be strengthened by emphasizing core competencies beyond technology: transformational leadership, information management, and change management. CIO assignment should be part of a career in leadership.[9]

Experimenting, Learning, and Evaluating

Another lesson lies in the need to promote local learning, innovation, and evaluation—all key ingredients of implementing digital transformation programs. Transformation demands stakeholder's engagement to innovate, adapt, and learn to realize the potential benefits of digital technologies. Transforming countries engage in pragmatic policy experimentation. Successful digital transformation strategies are not fixed blueprints or recipes. Inclusive transformation strategies and plans deploy a number of incentives and innovation funds to promote societal learning, diffuse ICT among small enterprises, invest in human resources for the information society, and promote societal applications that target marginalized groups. It is equally important to plan to learn as it is to learn to plan (Ellerman et al. 2001; Hanna 2011, 2016a, 2020).

Digital technologies present novel policy and regulatory challenges that require agility and experimentation. Lessons can be learned from pioneering countries about creating regulatory sandboxes for policy and regulatory innovations. These sandboxes allow live, time-bound testing of innovations under a regulator's oversight. They offer safe space to test new regulations and provide quick feedback on the feasibility and impact of these regulatory innovations before wide adoption at the national level.

Digital transformation requires extensive local learning. The Bank performed relatively well when technology was embedded in Bank funded Investment projects. These projects (mainly engineering and hardware oriented) were suited for blueprint design. They did not need as much local technological experimentation, adaptation, and learning. New technologies, however, require deep organizational, business process, and skills development to fit with the socio-technical context of a developing country. Digital dividends are conditioned by local policies, institutions, and skills (World Bank 2016; Hanna 2016). Bank assistance capacity and processes are being tested by these new technology transfer and technical assistance requirements.

[9] CIO should mean chief information or chief innovation officer, not Career Is Over!

Learning and acting at the same time are the essence of accelerated development and transformation. Pursuing digital transformation as an adaptive learning process encourages learning from pilots and sharing experience from successes and failures. This cannot be done only from the center, top down, or as a one-off event. Deliberate strategy, emphasizing focus and control, has to be complemented by emergent strategy, emphasizing continuous learning and venturing. An effective digital transformation process requires change management, institutionalized learning, user-driven innovation, and multiple feedback mechanisms. It also requires tools for managing and sharing knowledge, learning communities, and participatory monitoring and evaluation.

A mindset shift from sourcing universal best practices to "best fit" adaptation to the local context is required. Imposing off the-shelf-best practices or donor conditions for reforms is unlikely to succeed. Much of digital transformation practices must be experimented with, adapted to local context, owned by the stakeholders, and evaluated in situ.

A central task of pursuing digital transformation is learning at all levels: in government, business, and civil society sectors as well as academia. This is particularly essential for a new sector, for mastering a general-purpose technology. Singapore, for example, created a high-speed learning environment and made its economy a test-bed for digital innovation.

Digital transformation learning may focus on priority sectors where externalities spillover learning effects are high, and/or transformation is fundamental to the accelerated development of the whole economy. Some countries target the education sector for digital innovation as they view education as a pillar of the dynamic digital economy and an inclusive information society. Education, however, is a sector where innovation is slow to emerge and diffuse. Transformation of this sector requires the highest commitment to socio-technical innovation, shared learning, and change management.

Monitoring and evaluation (M&E) are perhaps the weakest elements of e-strategies in developing countries. Setting M&E systems for learning and indicators for measuring progress for e-strategies presents a dilemma. On the one hand, e-transformation is a novel and poorly-understood process, with profound implications for all sectors, and hence needs to be piloted and adapted in diverse local contexts, with much attention to innovation and learning. On the other hand, applying quantitative M&E systems and indicators to a new and poorly understood phenomenon runs the risk of measuring inputs rather than outcomes, emphasizing hard data over the soft but more relevant and critical information, and ignoring poorer regions and constituencies. Weak M&E systems have also led to heavy reliance on rigid and centralized plans for accountability, rather than local engagement and learning.

Decentralization and support to bottom-up initiatives can spur innovation, experimentation, and learning. Several mechanisms may be used to institutionalize and support bottom-up initiatives, such as, for example, matching grants and the e-Society program piloted in e-Sri Lanka (Hanna 2007, 2008). *InfoDev*, a donor funded program that the Bank administered between 1995 and 2015, intended to promote pilots and experimentation with the new digital technologies in developing countries. These kinds of mechanisms and the corresponding communities of practice they create can unleash a flood of ideas and energy. They can encourage small enterprises, and grassroots- and community-based organizations to engage with the national ICT agencies in linking to various parts of the national digital program. When appropriately targeted, they help the central agencies understand their most vulnerable clients—rural communities and the poor—and empower them to co-innovate local ICT solutions. However, these innovation funds should be oriented to spread and scale up the most promising innovations through support to local enabling institutions and societal learning processes.

The e-society program in the Sri Lanka case shows both the potential and limits of such grassroots innovation funds. It was built into the Sri Lanka digital strategy. While the program spawned many interesting digital and societal innovations, few were taken up subsequently for scaling by the private sector, government ministries, or aid agencies. Such programs were often sponsored and financed by external agencies, but were terminated once external funding stopped. Impact was also limited by poor knowledge management, marketing, and sharing of the learning generated from these pilots. Sustaining these programs called for public-private partnerships, and nurturing local institutions that would prioritize and manage innovations for adaptation and scaling up.

A promising approach to spur innovation and transformation in public service may come from enhanced transparency and demand for open governance and accountability, enabled by the use of digital technologies (Hanna 2017). Digital government, e-education, and other ICT applications in the public sector in developing countries tend to be supply driven. Some digital economy leaders started with supply-driven strategies, but have since moved to more demand mobilization and virtuous supply-demand cycles.

Continuous improvements in services and innovation in government processes require demand for performance. This demand can be strengthened by meaningful efforts to capture citizen feedback on services—devising the right metrics to measure results and account for innovation and continual service improvement. Appropriately applied, accountability to citizens can also promote innovative public-private partnerships. Grassroots organizations and social intermediaries can play a key role in mobilizing public will, political capital, and champions of social innovation to demand community-defined results. They can support experimentation, push for creative solutions, and counter risk aversion incentives. Using assessment frameworks and metrics that focus on results and deploying participatory processes that capture citizen feedback can be key drivers for innovation and accountability.

The recent trends in digital technologies offer powerful platforms for collaborative, networked, and grassroots innovation. Countries like Singapore and Estonia that started with a more top-down strategy have recently reoriented their strategies to rely on collaborative government and collaborative innovation. Government still steers the fundamentals such as developing an enabling policy environment, co-investing in broadband, using digital government as a platform for service innovation, and promoting public-private partnerships for innovation. Pioneering governments are learning to listen to clients, to seek partners, and to collaborate with all segments of society. This means re-learning skills and changing attitudes. The new collaborative technologies make the process easier, but changing attitudes, habits and practices takes time, persistence, leadership, and change management capabilities.

Prioritizing Inclusion and Diffusion

In my experience at the Bank, and subsequently in my engagement with leading technology companies, there was a common disconnect between the growing appreciation of the potential of digital technologies for growth and competitiveness on the one hand, and recognizing the impact of these technologies on economic inequality and poverty, on the other hand. As described earlier, the Bank's initial digital economy assessments gave little attention to this distributional impact. It focused mainly on creating isolated digital islands of excellence, leaving the rest of the economy in the dark. Advocacy for digital technology tends to gloss over these risks. Often countries make the case for digital transformation in support of poverty reduction and economic inclusion, yet have their digital agenda dominated by the interests of elite users, few connected urban centers, and powerful digital monopolies.

The distributional implications of the digital revolution are likely to be profound. Its distributional effects must be explicitly addressed, however difficult and messy they may be. Countries should at least avoid compounding the already high levels of income inequality in most developing countries. More ambitiously, they should leverage new technologies to develop cost-effective solutions to persistent development challenges, such as decent employment, social protection, education and health, and public services for the poor.

Digital technologies can be harnessed in to generate shared benefits for whole society. Digital investments that give jobs and other opportunities to the poor should matter as much as those lowering costs of goods and services and accelerating economic growth. That is often easier said than done. It requires a whole of government approach to job creation. It requires piloting and experimenting with policies and investments to appropriate the new technologies by and for the poor.

Inclusion is a cross-cutting policy area. It involves all elements of the digital transformation ecosystem. It is essential to design policy reforms and investments for all these elements to connect all economic and social groups to the opportunities generated by digitalization. Key tools are: universal digital connectivity, digital literacy, digital financial services, digital safeguards for vulnerable consumers, diffusion and extension programs for SMEs, and digital identification (ID).

Various means can be deployed to secure digital inclusion. Expanding network coverage continues to be a challenge in low income countries. A policy priority for these countries is to eliminate high entry barriers that limit competition and private investment in digital infrastructure. Also critical is to promote shared infrastructure arrangements to drive down costs and make services more affordable. But well-regulated markets must be complemented with targeted public policies to ensure universal digital access: investment incentives to cover marginal areas, public-private partnerships, well-calibrated demand-side and supply-side subsidies, among others. The Bank has not fully explored the potential developmental impact of telecenters (shared access or community information centers) for providing affordable access and digital literacy. Access to electricity may be a prerequisite for enabling usage of digital technologies, particularly in poor countries and isolated regions. Many countries have yet to exploit the cost savings from shared access to electricity and internet infrastructures.

Digital financial services are also a promising enabler for inclusion. The digital revolution has catalyzed increased access to financial services, transforming how people make and receive payments, borrow, and save. Digital transformation makes it easier, cheaper, and safer for people to receive wages from employers, send remittances to family members, and pay for goods and services. Mobile money accounts can better handle high-volume, small-denomination transactions, which help users to access financial services and save. Government social programs can now reduce delays and leakage by channeling transfers directly to their beneficiaries' mobile phones. Building on these encouraging trends is crucial.

Governments and the private sector can further accelerate this transformation. Regulation should ensure open and fair access to critical financial infrastructure and services. Policies to ensure social and gender inclusion in digital financial services would include extending financial consumer protection to the specific needs of target groups. They would also promote financial literacy programs covering skills relevant to the use of digital financial services. Cheap and functional mobile phones and affordable internet access are prerequisites for expanding digital finance. Establishing digital identification (e-ID) systems is essential to identity verification and access to financial services.

To ensure that digital transformation is both sustainable and equitable, effective country adopters of digital technologies strive to diffuse digital solutions and capture network externalities while at the same time closing the digital divide. Successful digital pioneers start at early stages with affordable internet access and universal digital literacy. The quest for jobs, opportunities, and income for the poor must go beyond the digital sector itself and cover digital applications across many human development and livelihood strategies. Given the wide gap in productivity between large enterprises and small and micro enterprises, digital diffusion programs should target these small enterprises to enhance their productivity and help access information and markets.

Countries have to experiment their way forward as distributional issues are contextual and difficult to solve. Developing countries may need to develop mechanisms to promote social and "frugal" innovation as well as affordable solutions that are co-innovated with the poor and their social intermediaries. They should also seek ways to integrate digital solutions into pro-poor policies and programs such as rural development, social protection and public works to enhance their effectiveness reach, and accountability. Overcoming the digital divide requires promoting pro-poor innovation and targeting digital diffusion to poor communities and regions. In India, for example, digital identification programs are building an inclusive platform for service delivery.

Forward to the Future

In this book, I shared my lessons of experience in driving digital transformation. They are summed up in five fundamentals—future orientation and continuity; empowerment and ownership; leadership, institutions, and human resources; experimentation and learning; and diffusion and inclusion. These fundamentals reinforce each other. Transformational leadership envisions the road ahead and builds consensus for the long term. Commitment to experimentation and learning helps maintain policy flexibility and avoid ideological lock-ins, while securing future orientation and sustained commitment to the long-term objectives of digital development. Digital inclusion has become essential to social cohesion and economic inclusion. It can be achieved through national consensus, innovation, and learning. In turn, widespread digital diffusion and its tangible benefits lend support to visionary leaders, robust institutions, private investment, and social consensus for pursuing transformation. They open possibilities for a virtuous cycle.

These five fundamentals are about the "how" to transform, or learning to transform. But what about the "why" to transform. The aims of transformation would vary across countries and would depend on a country's aspirations, comparative advantages, and stage in realizing their own sustainable development goals. Digital transformation can be directed to build responsive and inclusive public services, open and transparent government, smart cities, and resilient infrastructures. It can open opportunities for life-long learning and access to quality education. It enables the creation of globally competitive industries and quality jobs. Most broadly, it is about building learning organizations, learning society, and learning systems in priority economic sectors.

The versatility of digital technologies and their dependence on non-digital competencies and institutional complements suggest that digital strategies must become integral to country development strategies. It can be harnessed to enable new development strategies and discover new paths to development for the digital age. It is a core competency for society to thrive and navigate the challenges of local and global development. It is no longer the exclusive domain of a single ministry, agency, or discipline.

The digital revolution continues to sweep the world economy. Much of the impact of digital technologies is yet to be felt as we embrace the ever-expanding opportunities of data-driven and intelligence-driven innovation while building digital capabilities and coping with the pace of technological change and the associated risks. This revolution is still gathering steam—raising much hope and expectations.

What will the future look like? Our future will not be decided by data, internet, or artificial intelligence alone. Transformative technologies defy predictions. Hopefully, the future will be shaped by shared human values, culture, and creativity as digital technologies transform economies and relationships among government, business, civil society, and citizens. Developing countries need to imagine and anticipate the future to identify opportunities arising from the digital revolution. We need to rehearse the future to understand the risks and uncertainties ahead.

If we are to thrive in this future, we must focus on the critical foundations of leadership, governance, institutions, human resources, and culture needed for digital transformation. We need to adopt an inclusive ecosystem approach to digital transformation and learn to partner to govern the whole ecosystem.

Who should lead, own, and build a country's digital transformation ecosystem? It should be locally led, owned, and driven. Digital transformation is a process, not a blueprint. Local stakeholders should participate in the process of shaping this ecosystem toward a shared and desired future. A parallel process should take place within aid agencies—cutting across bureaucratic silos to provide support to the entire ecosystem based on a consensus about the use of digital technologies to respond to immediate crises while laying the long-term foundations for a desirable future.

Digital transformation calls for a new style of leadership that is central to profound, sustained, transformational change. This means leadership that is open, collaborative, and vision-driven. Managers must empower staff to learn, innovate, and serve clients. They must set free the substantial talent and creativity of their staff to co-create and empower ecosystem stakeholders.

The future is digital. The digital revolution opens a window of opportunity for countries to practice a new style of leadership that nurtures innovation and leverages new technologies to alleviate poverty and power sustainable development. Digital transformation must become a core competency for country leaders in the twenty-first century aiming to address the multiple crises and opportunities facing them and mankind.

Annex 1: Global Best Practices in Digital Transformation Strategy

An analysis of global best practices in the development and implementation of digital transformation strategies at the country, sub-regional and regional levels can be summarized in the following guidelines or checklist for policymakers.

Develop Leadership and Governance

Adopt a holistic vision and ecosystem approach

- Develop in-depth understanding of existing digital ecosystem—beyond silos
- Prioritize digital foundations over stand-alone applications
- Build consensus on a vision, driven by development priorities and opportunities
- Develop a sense of urgency and commitment to transformation
- Use holistic digital diagnostics to set realistic targets
- Develop synergies among ecosystem elements

Take a Long-term view, combined with agile implementation

- Encourage long-term thinking for outcomes and sustainability—marathon
- Capture low-hanging-fruits to build commitment and demonstrate quick payoff

N. K. Hanna, *Driving Digital Transformation in Developing Nations*, https://doi.org/10.1007/978-3-031-54573-3

- Build agile implementation capabilities and processes
- Phase digital transformation programs in line with augmented capabilities
- Develop medium-term investment plans and diversify sources of finance, including IFIs.

Develop digital leadership and institutions

- Build leadership institutions with clear roles and competencies
- Develop collaborative links with adopting sectors
- Build a cadre of digital transformation leaders—CDTOs
- Develop agile, independent regulatory agencies
- Balance central leadership with bottom-up innovation
- Build institutions for national, regional, and global cooperation.

Develop Policies, Regulations, Data, and Cybersecurity

- Develop enabling policies and safeguards to establish competition and trust
- Support and encourage reuse of open data, open standards, and open source
- Develop a whole-of-society cybersecurity and resilience strategies
- Invest in digital public goods, in partnership with business and civil society
- Develop AI policy and strategy to enable innovation, and accelerate adoption
- Promote integration of data and processes among public agencies
- Build geospatial information platforms for environmental resilience

Build Digital Infrastructure and Platforms

- Encourage competition to build backbone, and secure, affordable Internet service
- Adopt innovative institutional and financing mechanisms to drive access and usage
- Develop and regulate digital platforms for identification, commerce, finance, and services
- Prioritize mobile connectivity and cloud infrastructure

- Promote sharing of infrastructure and spectrum
- Promote network interconnection and interoperability of services and platforms
- Promote partnerships for digital platforms in priority areas
- Promote open public platforms to serve both the delivery of government services and as common platform for innovation and delivery of private sector services

Develop Skills and Competencies

- Promote universal digital literacy and skills through education systems and enterprises
- Develop analytics, artificial intelligence, and data management capabilities
- Develop centres of excellence for digital capacity development
- Develop, attract, and retain digital talents in public and private sector
- Develop tailored and sustainable training systems for civil servants
- Integrate digital education into management programs
- Promote digital academies, competence centres, and apprenticeship schemes
- Promote digitally enabled learning at all education levels

Promote ICT Sector, Innovation, and Finance

Develop the digital sector to support local transformation

- Develop a competitive digital services industry for jobs and ecosystem dynamism
- Prioritize digital sector mission as key enabler for transforming whole economy
- Advance "ease of doing business" for dynamic digital services
- Develop public–private partnerships to promote a competitive digital industry
- Promote export strategies for digital services in partnership with industry associations
- Adopt appropriate international standards and best practices in public procurement of ICT

- Promote the development of digitized, development-relevant local content

Promote innovation and finance for transformation

- Nurture innovation and entrepreneurship ecosystems—demand-led techno-parks
- Develop programs to scale up and diffuse digital innovations among SMEs
- Set priorities, pilots, and safeguards for emerging technologies
- Prioritize inclusive and frugal innovation, and develop grassroots innovation networks
- Promote access to finance for digital startups and SMEs
- Promote digital financial literacy.
- Promote FinTech in mobile, digital payment, money transfer, banking.

Transform Business and Public Sectors

Develop ICT-enabled economy and sector-wide transformation strategies

- Align digital strategy with country economic development strategies.
- Prioritize adoption capabilities in key user clusters–adopt sector-wide approaches
- Promote digital transformation of SMEs via business associations and local governments
- Emphasize sustainable, scalable, sector-wide digital applications
- Provide sector-specific complementary investments and training to maximize digital dividends
- Target country and regional comparative advantages for accelerated transformation.
- Prioritize "intelligent" infrastructure for sustainability: smart transport, energy, cities.
- Promote e-trade particularly in digital services and products
- Develop digital platforms for the transforming sectors

Engineer effective adoption of digital government

- Develop digital government vision, strategy, and implementation roadmap.
- Use digital government as a platform for data, services, and public–private partnership
- Mobilize demand for good government and improved public services
- Adopt a whole-of-government approach for digitizing core systems and key services
- Digitize country registries covering citizens, business, and land.
- Support local initiatives for digitized local government services
- Use digital government for transparency and accountability.
- Adopt best practices in e-gov: single window, interoperability, user-centric, multi-channels, etc.

Cross-Cutting Goals (Principles)

Promote digital inclusion

- Address the digital divide and pre-existing inequalities
- Use shared access, community centres and low-cost channels to reach low-resource settings
- Identify and stimulate nascent demand in lagging regions—local content
- Promote digital culture and literacy to secure wide and effective adoption
- Prioritize affordable access and build transformation capabilities of small business
- Build informational capabilities of social intermediaries and marginalized communities
- Prioritize youth and women for wide developmental impact

Promote ownership and partnerships

- Build broad multi-stakeholder ownership and participation
- Create digital platforms for consultation, collaboration, and project generation
- Develop strategic communication strategy to generate national consensus
- Build partnerships, among stakeholders, across sectors, at all levels, and over time

- Develop and partner with private ICT services associations
- Build capacity of weak stakeholders to participate effectively
- Develop country-led forums for digital cooperation with development finance partners.
- Invest in collaborative tools among universities, suppliers, and users.

Maximize learning and adaptation

- Shift from rigid blueprint plans to adaptive, learning, results-driven strategies.
- Capture local knowledge and grassroots innovations–develop scaling up mechanisms
- Balance central direction with local initiative– Integrate local learning into strategies
- Build foresight capabilities—scan and prepare for disruptive technologies
- Focus research on adoption, evaluation, and outcomes
- Engage local universities and think tanks in locally relevant, applied research.
- Keep score through timely monitoring and evaluation—multiple feedback.
- Develop the statistical benchmarks of the digital economy
- Create platforms and centres of excellence to capture and diffuse best practice.

My Relevant Publications

Hanna, Nagy. 1985. *Strategic Planning and Management*, World Bank Discussion Paper. Washington DC: World Bank. https://documents.worldbank.org/en/publication/documents-reports/documentdetail/562811468765919659/strategic-planning-and-management-a-review-of-recent-experience.

———. 1990. *Development in the Information Age: An Evolving Role for the World Bank*. World Bank, memio.

———. 1991. *The Information Technology Revolution and Economic Development*. World Bank Discussion Paper 120. Washington DC: World Bank. https://elibrary.worldbank.org/doi/abs/10.1596/0-8213-1784-9.

———. 2007a. *From Envisioning to Designing e-Development: The Experience of Sri Lanka*. World Bank. http://documents.worldbank.org/curated/en/438421468104642480/From-envisioning-to-designing-e-development-the-experience-of-Sri-Lanka.

———. 2007b. *e-Leadership Institutions for the Knowledge Economy*. Washington, DC: World Bank.

———. 2008. *Transforming Government and Empowering Communities: The Sri Lanka Experience*. Directions in Development Series. Washington, DC: World Bank. https://openknowledge.worldbank.org/handle/10986/6345?locale-attribute=en.

———. 2009. *e-Transformation: Enabling New Development Strategies*. New York: Springer.

———. 2010. *Transforming Government and Building the Information Society*. New York: Springer.

———. 2011. *Enabling Enterprise Transformation: Business and Grassroots Innovation for the Knowledge Economy*. New York: Springer.

N. K. Hanna, *Driving Digital Transformation in Developing Nations*,
https://doi.org/10.1007/978-3-031-54573-3

———. 2012a. *Open, Smart, and Inclusive Development: ICT for Transforming North Africa*. Abidjan: African Development Bank.

———. 2012b. *Transforming to a Networked Society: Guide for Policy Makers*. Maryland: Sriban. 2015.

———. 2016a. *Mastering Digital Transformation*. UK: Emerald.

———. 2017. *How Can Digital Technologies Improve Public Services and Governance?* New York, NY: Business Expert Press.

———. 2016. Thinking about Digital Dividends. *Information Technology & International Development* 12 (3): 25–30. A Review and Critique of the WBR2016: *Digital Dividends*.

———. 2018. Role of the State in the Digital Age. *Journal of Innovation and Entrepreneurship* 7 (1): 5. https://doi.org/10.1186/s13731-018-0086-3, New York: Springer.

———. 2020. Assessing the Digital Economy. *Journal of Innovation and Entrepreneurship* 9 (1): 16. https://doi.org/10.1186/s13731-020-00129-1.

Hanna, Nagy and Sandor Boyson. 1993. *Information Technology in World Bank lending: Increasing the Developmental Impact*. World Bank Discussion Paper.

Hanna, Nagy, K. Guy, and Arnold. 1995. *The Diffusion of Information Technology: Experience of Industrial Countries and Lessons for Developing Countries*. World Bank Discussion Paper.

Hanna, N.K., S. Boyson, and S. Gunaratne. 1996. *The East Asian Miracle and Information Technology: Strategic Management of Technological Learning*. World Bank Discussion Paper.

Ellerman, D., S. Denning, and N.K. Hanna. 2001. Active Learning and Development Assistance in Tacit Knowledge Exchange and Active Learning. Special issue. *Journal of Knowledge Management* 5 (2): 171–179.

Hanna, Nagy, and Peter Knight. 2011a. *Seeking Transformation through Information Technology: Strategies for Brazil, China, Canada and Sri Lanka*. New York: Springer.

Hanna, Nagy, and Peter Knight. 2011b. *National Strategies to Harness Information Technology: Seeking Transformation in Singapore, Finland, the Philippines, and South Africa*. New York: Springer.

Hanna, Nagy and C. Qiang. 2009. Trends in National E-Government Institutions. Information and Communications for Development. 2009. *Extending Reach and Increasing Impact*, 2009. Washington, DC: The World Bank.

———. 2010. China's Informatization Strategy. *International Experience in e-Development*. Washington DC: World Bank.

Hanna, Nagy, et al. 2000. *1999 Annual Review of Development Effectiveness*. World Bank Operations Evaluation Department. World Bank.

Hanna, Nagy, and Robert Picciotto, eds. 2002. *Making Development Work*. New Brunswick, NJ: Transaction Publishers.

References

Acemoğlu, D. and J.A. Robinson. 2012. *Why Nations Fail: The Origins of Power, Prosperity, and Poverty*. Crown Currency.

Amsden, Alice. 1989. *Asia's Next Giant: South Korea and Late Industrialization*. New York: Oxford University Press.

Argyris, Chris and Schon, Donald 1974. *Theory in Practice: increasing Professional Effectiveness*. Jossey-Bass Publishers

Asian Development Bank. 2022. CAREC Digital Strategy 2030: Accelerating Digital Transformation for Regional Competitiveness and Inclusive Growth. *ADB*, 2022.

Ayres, R.U. 1989. *Technological Transformation and Long Waves*. International Institute for Applied Systems Analysis. Research Report 98–1.

Brynjolfsson, E., and A. Saunders. 2010. *Wired for Innovation: How Information Technology is Reshaping the Economy*. Boston, MA: MIT Press.

Brynjolfsson, E., and McAfee, Andrew. 2017. *Machine, Platform, Crowd*. New York, NY: Norton & Company.

Carr, Nicholas. 2004. *Does IT Matter? Information Technology and the Corrosion of Competitive Advantage*. Boston: Harvard Business School Press.

Commission on Growth and Development. 2008. *The Growth Report: Strategies for Sustained Growth and Inclusive Development*. Washington, DC: World Bank.

Dahlman, Routti and Yla-Anttila. 2006. *Finland as a Knowledge Economy*. Washington D.C.: World Bank.

Davies, Richard. 2019. *Extreme Economies*. Great Britain: Bantam Press.

Dercon, Stefan. 2022. *Gambling on Development: Why Some Countries Win and Others Lose*. London: Hurst and Company.

Easterly, William. 2015. *The Tyranny of Experts: Economists, Dictators, and the Forgotten Rights of the Poor*. NY: Basic Books.

Easterly, W. 2007. *The White Man's Burden: Why the West's Efforts to Aid the Rest Have Done So Much Ill and So Little Good*. Oxford University Press.

Ellerman, David. 2002. Helping People help Themselves: Autonomy-compatible Assistance. In *Making Development Work*, ed. Hanna and Picciotto. New Brunswick, NJ: Transaction Publishers.

Evans, Peter. 1995. *Embedded Autonomy: States and Industrial Transformation*. Princeton, NJ: Princeton University Press.

Goldman, M., H. Ergas, E. Ralf, and G. Felker. 2013. *Technology Institutions and Policies*. World Bank.

Gurin, J. 2013. *Open Data Now*. McGraw-Hill Education.

Harari, Yuval. 2019. *21 Lessons for the 21st Century*. New York: Spiegel & Grau.

Hirschman, Albert O. 1958. *The Strategy for Economic Development*. New Haven: Yale University Press.

———. 1967 and 2002. *Development Projects Observed*. Brookings Institution.

ITU. 2010. *National e-Strategies for Development: Global Status and Prospects, 2010.*

Khanna, Ro. 2023. *Progressive Capitalism.* USA: Simon & Schuster.

Karnik, Kiran. 2012. *The Coalition of Competitors.* New Delhi: Collins Business.

Katz, Raul, and Fernando Callorda. (2018). *The Economic Contribution of Broadband, Digitization, and ICT Regulation.* Geneva, Switzerland: International Telecommunications Union.

———. (2020). *The Economic Contribution of Broadband, Digitization, and ICT Regulation: Econometric Modelling for Arab States.* Geneva, Switzerland: International Telecommunications Union.

Kaufmann, Daniel. 2002. *Rethinking Governance.* World Bank Institute. World Bank. Washington DC: December.

Komninos, N. 2008. *Intelligent Cities and Globalization of Innovation Networks.* Routledge.

Lall, Sanjay. 2004. *Reinvesting Industrial Strategy: The Role of Government Policy in Building Industrial Competitiveness.* G-24 Discussion Paper No. 28. United Nations, Geneva, April.

Mehta, Harish. 2022. *The Inside Story of a Movement that Shaped India's IT Revolution.* Harper Business India.

Melhem, Samia, and Astrid Herdis Jacobsen. 2022. *A Global Study on Digital Capabilities.* Washington, D.C.: World Bank Group.

Ndulu, Benno, Elizabeth Stuart, Stefan Dercon, and Peter Knaack. 2023. *Driving Digital Transformation: Lessons from Seven Developing Countries.* New York: Oxford University Press.

Nelson, Richard R. 2004. *The Changing Institutional Requirements for Technological Catch Up.* Columbia University, June.

North, Douglass C. 1990. *Institutions, Institutional Change and Economic Performance.* New York: Cambridge University Press.

Perez, Carlota. 2002. *Technological Revolutions and Financial Capital.* Cheltenham: Edward Elgar.

Rodrik, Dani. 2007. *One Economics, Many Recipes.* Princeton: Princeton University.

Sabel, Charles F. and Sanjay Reddy. N.d. *Learning to Learn: Undoing the Gordian Knot of Development Today.* Colombia University.

Sachs, Jeffrey. 2014. *The Age of Sustainable Development.* New York: Columbia University Press.

Saxenian, Anna Lee. 2002. *The New Argonauts: How Entrepreneurs are Linking Technology Markets in a Global Economy.* Cambridge: Harvard University Press.

Schmidt, Eric, and Jared Cohen. 2014. *The New Digital Age.* New York: Vintage Books.

Sen, Amartya. 2000. *Development as Freedom.* Anchor Books Edition.

Spence, Michael. 2011. *The Next Convergence*. New York: Farrar, Straus and Giroux.

Southwood, R. 2022. *Africa 2.0: Inside a Continent's Communications Revolution*. Manchester University Press.

Stiglitz, Joseph, and Bruce Greenwold. 2014. *Creating a Learning Society*. New York: Columbia University Press.

Tapscott, Don. 1997. *The Digital Economy : Promise And Peril In The Age Of Networked Intelligence*. New York: McGraw-Hill.

Tapscott, Don, and Anthony D. Williams. 2010. *Macrowikinomics: Rebooting Business and the World*. New York: Penguin Group.

Townsend, Anthony M. 2013. *Smart Cities*. New York: W.W. Norton & Company.

UNCTAD. 2013. *The Information Economy Report 2013: The Cloud Economy and Developing Countries*. New York: UN.

———. 2016. *Issues Paper on Foresight for Digital Development*. UNCTAD.

———. 2019. *Digital Economy Report 2019: Value Creation and Capture: Implications for Developing Countries*, New York: UN, https://doi.org/10.18356/c7dc937a-en.

United Nations (UN). *E-government Surveys:* 2010, 2012, 2014, 2016, 2018. http://unpan1.un.org/intradoc/groups/public/documents/un/unpan047965.pdf.

Unwin, T. 2017. *Reclaiming Information & Communication Technologies for Development*. Oxford University Press.

Wade, Robert. 1990. *Governing the Market*. Princeton, NJ: Princeton University Press.

World Bank. 1993. *The East Asia Miracle: Economic Growth and Public Policies*. New York: Oxford University Press.

Wade, Robert. 1998. *Beyond the Washington Consensus: Institutions Matter*. Washington, DC: World Bank.

World Bank. Internal Audit Department (IAD). 1998. *Report on Follow up Review of Informatics*. Washington, DC: World Bank.

World Bank. 1999. *Knowledge for Development, World Development Report 1998–99*. Washington, DC: World Bank.

———. 2009. *Information and Communications for Development 2009. Extending Reach and Increasing Impact*. Washington, DC: World Bank.

———. 2012a. *ICT for Greater Development Impact: World Bank Group Strategy for Information and Communication Technology*. Washington, DC: World Bank.

———. 2012b. *Maximizing Mobile*. Washington DC: World Bank.

———. 2014. *Independent Evaluation Group. Implementation Completion and Results Report for E-Sri Lanka Project*. September 17, 2014. Washington DC: World Bank.

World Bank. World Development Report. 2016. *Digital Dividends*. Washington DC: World Bank.

World Bank. 2017. Kelly, Tim, Liaplina, Aleksandra, Tan, Shawn W., Winkler, Hernan. *Reaping Digital Dividends: Leveraging the Internet for Development in Europe and Central Asia. Europe and Central Asia Studies.* Washington, DC: World Bank.

———. 2018a. *Competing in the Digital Age: Policy Implications for the Russian Federation*. Washington DC: World Bank.

———. 2018b. *Malaysia's Digital Economy: A New Driver for Development.* Washington DC: World Bank.

———. 2019a. *Nigeria Digital Economy Diagnostic Report.* Washington DC: World Bank.

———. 2019b. *Data-Driven Development*. Washington DC: World Bank.

———. 2021. *Mobilizing Technology for Development: An assessment of World Bank Group Preparedness.* Independent Evaluation Group. Washington, DC: World Bank.

———. 2022a. Cruz, Marcio, Dutz, Mark A., Rodríguez-Castelán, Carlos. *Digital Senegal for Inclusive Growth: Technological Transformation for Better and More Jobs.* Washington, DC: World Bank.

———. 2022b. *South Asia's Digital Opportunity: Accelerating Growth, Transforming Lives.* Washington, DC: World Bank.

World Economic Forum. 2012. *Big Data, Big Impact: New Possibilities for International Development*.

———. 2015. *The Global Information Technology Report 2015*. World Economic Forum.

Index

N. K. Hanna, *Driving Digital Transformation in Developing Nations*, https://doi.org/10.1007/978-3-031-54573-3

The manufacturer's authorised representative in the EU is Springer Nature Customer Service Centre GmbH, Europaplatz 3, 69115 Heidelberg, Germany. If you have any concerns regarding our products, please contact ProductSafety@springernature.com

Printed and bound by CPI Group (UK) Ltd, Croydon, CR0 4YY
30/09/2026
02225565-0002